University of Michigan
Ann Arbor, Michigan

Written by Michael Hondorp

Edited by Alexis Fabrikant, Adam Burns,
and Kimberly Moore

Additional contributions by Omid Gohari,
Christina Koshzow, Chris Mason, Joey Rahimi,
and Luke Skurman

D0003665

ISBN # 1-59658-163-8
ISSN # 1551-115x
© Copyright 2005 College Prowler
All Rights Reserved
Printed in the U.S.A.
www.collegeprowler.com

Last updated on 10/25/05

Special thanks to: Babs Carryer, Andy Hannah, LaunchCyte, Tim O'Brien, Bob Sehlinger, Thomas Emerson, Andrew Skurman, Barbara Skurman, Bert Mann, Dave Lehman, Daniel Fayock, Chris Babyak, The Donald H. Jones Center for Entrepreneurship, Terry Slease, Jerry McGinnis, Bill Ecenberger, Idie McGinty, Kyle Russell, Jacque Zaremba, Larry Winderbaum, Roland Allen, Jon Reider, Team Evankovich, Lauren Varacalli, Abu Noaman, Mark Exler, Daniel Steinmeyer, Jared Cohon, Gabriela Oates, David Koegler, and Glen Meakem.

Bounce-Back Team: Brian Netter, Kelly Kandra, and Katie Waller

College Prowler®
5001 Baum Blvd.
Suite 750
Pittsburgh, PA 15213

Phone: 1-800-290-2682
Fax:1-800-772-4972
E-mail: info@collegeprowler.com
Web Site: www.collegeprowler.com

Welcome to College Prowler®

During the writing of College Prowler's guidebooks, we felt it was critical that our content was unbiased and unaffiliated with any college or university. We think it's important that our readers get honest information and a realistic impression of the student opinions on any campus—that's why if any aspect of a particular school is terrible, we (unlike a campus brochure) intend to publish it. While we do keep an eye out for the occasional extremist—the cheerleader or the cynic—we take pride in letting the students tell it like it is. We strive to create a book that's as representative as possible of each particular campus. Our books cover both the good and the bad, and whether the survey responses point to recurring trends or a variation in opinion, these sentiments are directly and proportionally expressed through our guides.

College Prowler guidebooks are in the hands of students throughout the entire process of their creation. Because you can't make student-written guides without the students, we have students at each campus who help write, randomly survey their peers, edit, layout, and perform accuracy checks on every book that we publish. From the very beginning, student writers gather the most up-to-date stats, facts, and inside information on their colleges. They fill each section with student quotes and summarize the findings in editorial reviews. In addition, each school receives a collection of letter grades (A through F) that reflect student opinion and help to represent contentment, prominence, or satisfaction for each of our 20 specific categories. Just as in grade school, the higher the mark the more content, more prominent, or more satisfied the students are with the particular category.

Once a book is written, additional students serve as editors and check for accuracy even more extensively. Our bounce-back team—a group of randomly selected students who have no involvement with the project—are asked to read over the material in order to help ensure that the book accurately expresses every aspect of the university and its students. This same process is applied to the 200-plus schools College Prowler currently covers. Each book is the result of endless student contributions, hundreds of pages of research and writing, and countless hours of hard work. All of this has led to the creation of a student information network that stretches across the nation to every school that we cover. It's no easy accomplishment, but it's the reason that our guides are such a great resource.

When reading our books and looking at our grades, keep in mind that every college is different and that the students who make up each school are not uniform—as a result, it is impor-tant to assess schools on a case-by-case basis. Because it's impossible to summarize an entire school with a single number or description, each book provides a dialogue, not a decision, that's made up of 20 different topics and hundreds of student quotes. In the end, we hope that this guide will serve as a valuable tool in your college selection process. Enjoy!

OMID GOHARI ◯ CHRISTINA KOSHZOW ◯ CHRIS MASON ◯ JOEY RAHIMI ◯ LUKE SKURMAN ◯
The College Prowler Team

UNIVERSITY OF MICHIGAN
Table of Contents

Introduction from the Author

When it came time to choose a college, I found myself in quite a dilemma. My innate indecisiveness played a large role in my inability to choose a school, but there were many factors at stake. Basically, I was looking for the perfect college experience. I wanted to be challenged by leading scholars, to choose from hundreds of student organizations in which I could be involved, and to cheer on national champion sports teams, all while living in the perfect town.

When I was finally forced to decide, the school that simply had it all was the University of Michigan. Nowhere else could I find a better mix of academics, opportunities, sports, and atmosphere. Just like that, my decision was made.

I had never considered a large school until I realized what Michigan had to offer. Its size seemed daunting at first, but soon enough I found myself in classes with fewer than 20 students, cheering the football team on with my new friends, and being a member of a national award-winning a cappella group.

My experiences at Michigan showed me the world. Not only in the literal sense—as I studied in Spain, and toured the continent of Australia—but I saw the world through the eyes of my fellow students who came from backgrounds more diverse than I had ever known. Because of Michigan's unparalleled diversity, I learned just as much outside of the classroom as I learned inside of it. However, in the class, my eyes were opened, as well. Nearly every academic program is rated in the top 10 in the nation, and that's easy to realize when you're taking classes from the most famous scholars in a particular field. In addition, undergraduates have amazing opportunities to participate in the types of groundbreaking research that graduate students from other state schools could only dream of experiencing.

Admittedly, my college decision was difficult, but choosing Michigan was the best decision I have ever made. I was once worried about where I'd be for the next four years, but as soon as I moved to Ann Arbor, my worries subsided, and the greatest four years of my life began.

If you're looking for superior academics, countless opportunities, unparalleled athletics, and a worldwide reputation all set in a quintessential college town, look no further. The University of Michigan has it all. Best of luck, and Go Blue!

Michael Hondorp, Author
University of Michigan

By the Numbers

General Information

University of Michigan
Ann Arbor, MI 48109

Control:
Public

Academic Calendar:
Trimester

Religious Affiliation:
None

Founded:
1817

Web Site:
http://www.umich.edu

Main Phone:
(734) 764-1817

Admissions Phone:
(734) 764-7433

Student Body

**Full-Time
Undergraduates:**
23,773

**Part-Time
Undergraduates:**
1,055

**Total Male
Undergraduates:**
12,216

**Total Female
Undergraduates:**
12,612

Admissions

Overall Acceptance Rate:
62%

Total Applicants:
21,293

Total Acceptances:
13,304

Freshman Enrollment:
6,037

Yield (% of admitted students who actually enroll):
42%

Early Decision Available?
No

Early Action Available?
No

Regular Decision Deadline:
February 1

Regular Decision Notification:
Modified rolling
(approximately 12-14 weeks)

Must Reply-By Date:
May 1

Applicants Placed on Waiting List:
4,836

Applicants Accepted from Waiting List:
5

Transfer Applications Received:
2,575

Transfer Applicants Accepted:
1,023

Transfer Students Enrolled:
836

Transfer Application Acceptance Rate:
25%

Common Application Accepted?
No

Supplemental Forms?
Portfolio for art students, Audition for music students

Admissions E-mail:
ugadmiss@umich.edu

Admissions Web Site:
http://www.admissions.umich.edu

SAT I or ACT Required?
Yes

**First-Year Students
Submitting SAT Scores:**
58%

**SAT I Range
(25th–75th Percentile):**
1210–1400

**SAT I Verbal Range
(25th–75th Percentile):**
580–680

**SAT I Math Range
(25th–75th Percentile):**
630–720

Retention Rate:
95%

**Top 10% of
High School Class:**
90%

Application Fee:
$40

Financial Information

In-State Tuition:
$8,910

Out-of-State Tuition:
$27,129

Room and Board:
$7,374

Books and Supplies:
$980 per year

**Average Need-Based
Financial Aid Package
(including loans, work-study,
grants, and other sources):**
$11,306

**Students Who
Applied For Financial Aid:**
55%

Students Who Received Aid:
44%

**Financial Aid Forms
Deadline:**
February 15

Financial Aid Phone:
(764) 763-6600

Financial Aid E-mail:
financial.aid@umich.edu

Financial Aid Web Site:
http://www.finaid.umich.edu

Academics

The Lowdown On...
Academics

Degrees Awarded:
Bachelor
Master
Doctorate

Most Popular Majors:
17% Engineering
10% Psychology
 9% Economics
 8% Political Scince
 7% English Language
 6% Literature

Fulltime Faculty:
2,197

Faculty with Terminal Degree:
95%

Student-to-Faculty Ratio:
15:1

Average Course Load:
Four or five classes

➜

Undergraduate Schools:

College of Literature, Science, and the Arts (LSA)*

College of Architecture and Urban Planning

School of Art and Design*

School of Business Administration

School of Education

College of Engineering*

School of Kinesiology*

School of Music*

School of Nursing*

School of Pharmacy

*Schools that freshmen can apply to

AP Test Score Requirements:

Possible credit for scores of 4 or 5

IB Test Score Requirements:

Possible credit for scores of 6 or 7

Graduation Rates:

Four-Year: 67%

Five-Year: 84%

Six-Year: 87%

Did You Know?

Freshman seminars, which have fewer than 20 students, are reported to be among **the most rewarding academic experiences**. There are dozens from which to choose, including titles such as "I, Too, Sing America: Prejudice and Racism in American Society," and "The African Francophone."

Make sure not to step on the "M" in the center of the Diag (center of campus). It's said that if you do, you'll fail your first bluebook exam.

Michigan has **the largest alumni population** of any school in the world, with over 425,000 living alumni.

Best Places to Study:

Law Library, Grad Library Reading Room, UGLi (pronounced "ugly," stands for undergraduate library)

Students Speak Out On...
Academics

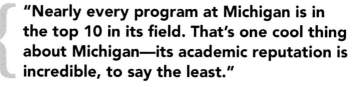

"Nearly every program at Michigan is in the top 10 in its field. That's one cool thing about Michigan—its academic reputation is incredible, to say the least."

Q "The professors are awesome here. The Graduate Student Instructors (GSIs) get **totally mixed reviews**. You just have to be proactive and switch your class if you don't like the teacher."

Q "Your academic experience at UM depends on what school you're in. In the College of Engineering, **it's hit or miss**. I've had horrible professors, and I've had great ones. A lot of foreign teachers don't speak English very well. Most of your time will probably be spent not with the teachers, but with the GSIs. The same goes for them; it's hit or miss."

Q "The UROP (Undergraduate Research Opportunity Program) is amazing. It gives undergraduates the opportunity to do **ground-breaking research** with renowned professors and present their research at the end of the year. Maybe you'll win a medal!"

Q "The quality of teachers varies greatly across the University, so it pays to do your research before registering for classes. By and large, I was able to learn from professors who had **genuine interest in teaching** and who could make even the dullest subject matter seem exciting. I also learned that getting to know the professors outside of class was well worth the effort."

Q "Professors at Michigan are okay. I mean, I had a couple of really good ones. Remember that the school is huge, so there are a whole of lot of professors. For the most part, there are not really bad ones, but there are some really difficult classes (Elie Wiesel, for example, teaches classes in the University Professors, theology, and Core). Unfortunately, **the most renowned professors aren't very accessible**, and they have graduate assistants that do all the grading. It's a big school, and that's just the way it is. But I have had some excellent professors who really care about their students and are very available. And some of the grad students aren't that bad either. They can be very good resources."

Q "I've had some good experiences with good teachers and some bad experiences with some bad ones. During freshman year, you'll get mostly graduate students teaching smaller breakdowns of the large lectures. Many of these **grad student teachers simply aren't ready**. However, I find that, as I get older, the quality of the teaching only goes up."

Q "**Be ready to work hard**. This school has no remedial classes, and because they know that students are smart, professors expect you to do a lot of work."

Q "Most of the teachers here are phenomenal—except for first-year calculus GSIs. A lot of the intro math courses are so large that real professors can't teach them. They hire grad students to teach the courses, and a lot of times **they can't speak English**. This is the biggest problem at the University. I would ask around, especially before registering for second-semester classes where you can definitely get the better professors. I've had some great, world-renowned professors who have made a difference in my education."

Q "My program, musical theatre, is known as **one of the top three in the country**. We have amazing professors with incredible credentials, and we have workshops with some of the biggest names on Broadway quite often."

Q "I went to the Mechanical Engineering school and the teachers there were great. I was always able to talk to them by **going to office hours**. My non-engineering classes were usually very large, and I had less contact with the teachers. Some classes were excellent, and others were just okay."

Q "Overall, I'd say academics here are pretty good. I'm in kinesiology, and I've taken courses in the business school and LSA. I've had good professors in each school, but **none of them will coddle you** at all. As long as you're on top of your stuff, teachers will respect you, and it will be apparent with your grades."

Q "My business school professors are amazing. Since our BBA program was rated number one a few years ago (and it's been in the top three ever since), the quality of education is great. Business school professors are a **mix of academic and working professionals**. It's a pretty good mix, too."

The College Prowler Take On...
Academics

At any major research university, one is bound to take classes taught by baby-faced grad students who didn't necessarily come to teach. At Michigan, this certainly holds true. GSIs (Michigan-speak for TAs), for the most part, are not well liked, but some students seem to luck out with a young, starry-eyed prodigy every once in a while. At a school the caliber of UM, the brilliant professors far outweigh the egotistical, narrow-minded ones. Even with some less-than-stellar GSIs, everyone agrees that UM's academics are first-rate.

Students are bound to have quite a sampling of professors, here. Sure, you'll have an unenthused GSI now and again for staple courses such as calculus, but there are more good professors than bad, and GSIs only teach discussion sections of larger lectures. Although you'd expect some of the best experiences to be found in small classes such as seminars (of which there are plenty), some large lectures have surprisingly engaging professors. Students pack the lectures halls and fill the hallways outside simply to catch a Ralph Williams lecture on Shakespeare or the Bible as literature. Simply stated, at a school as reputable as the University of Michigan, you are bound to find amazing professors who really care about teaching. They may have even written the book for the class you're taking.

B+

The College Prowler® Grade on
Academics: B+

A high Academics grade generally indicates that Professors are knowledgeable, accessible, and genuinely interested in their students' welfare. Other determining factors include class size, how well professors communicate, and whether or not classes are engaging.

Local Atmosphere

The Lowdown On...
Local Atmosphere

Region:
Midwest

City, State:
Ann Arbor, Michigan

Setting:
Small to medium-sized city
(about 114,000 residents)

Distance from Detroit:
1 hour

Distance from Chicago:
4 hours

Points of Interest:
Arboretum
Hands-on Museum
Museum of Art
Museum of Natural History
Wave Field on North Campus

➜

Closest Shopping Malls:

Briarwood Mall

Main Street (downtown)

State Street (on campus)

Closest Movie Theatres:

Michigan Theatre
(on campus)
603 East Liberty Street
Ann Arbor, MI
Type: Independent films, foreign films

State Theatre
(on campus)
233 S. State Street
Ann Arbor, MI
Type: Independent films, foreign films

Showcase Cinemas
4100 Carpenter Road
Ypsilanti, MI
Type: Multi-screen cineplex

Goodrich Quality 16
3686 Jackson Road
Ann Arbor, MI
Type: Multi-screen cineplex

Major Sports Teams:

Detroit Lions (football)

Detroit Pistons (basketball)

Detroit Tigers (baseball)

Detroit Red Wings (hockey)

City Web Sites

www.annarborfamily.com and www.annarbor.org are two great sites for details on various city events. You can find tourist and visitor information, as well as listings of interesting places to check out.

Did You Know

Fun Facts about Ann Harbor:

- It was labeled by environmentalists as **"Tree City USA."**

- The city was named one of the top 10 "**Best Places to Live**" by *Money* magazine.

- It's home to the biggest stadium in the nation, Michigan Stadium, which holds **over 110,000 Wolverine fans**.

Local Slang:
The "Big House" - Michigan Stadium

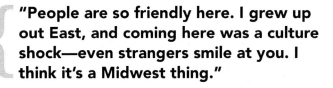

> "People are so friendly here. I grew up out East, and coming here was a culture shock—even strangers smile at you. I think it's a Midwest thing."

Q "Ann Arbor is a really fun town. The **people are really friendly**, and there's always something to do whether you want to see a movie, hear a concert, go out to dinner, catch a play, or hit the museums. Ann Arbor really has anything you want to do."

Q "Ann Arbor is a city in its own right, but life is dominated by UM. There are other universities nearby, but there is so much to do in Ann Arbor that there's no real need to go elsewhere. **Detroit is a wasteland**, unless you're going to the casino or something. Also, many underage students take the short trip to Windsor, Ontario, to take advantage of Canadian liquor laws. It's probably worth a one-time trip."

Q "It's **the perfect college town**. I don't ever want to leave. I mean ever!"

Q "Ann Arbor is pretty much **dependent on the University** of Michigan—it's a great place, regardless. Eastern Michigan University is nearby, but their students don't really come to Ann Arbor that often."

Q "Ann Arbor is a great town, and there really is no reason to leave. Detroit is 45 minutes away, but the only reason I would advise going there is to see a professional football, basketball, baseball, or hockey game. **I heard the casinos weren't bad** either. "

Q "There are no other universities in Ann Arbor, but nearby are Concordia College, Washtenaw Community College, Eastern Michigan U, and one more I can't think of. There are **tons of things to do**, and we have a decent public transportation system, as well."

Q "Ann Arbor is the best. I grew up in a very small town, so this city seems so cosmopolitan. **The opportunities here seem endless**."

Q "Well, **Ann Arbor is a college town**, make no mistake about it. Take advantage of the shows that come to Hill Auditorium. A lot of people visit Michigan State because it is supposedly a bigger party school than UM, and that's about 45 minutes away. You are four hours away from Chicago and Toronto, three hours from Cincinnati, and 45 minutes from Detroit."

Q "Sometimes I find myself wishing that I were back home in New York City. The **people here are too nice**. It's scary!"

Q "Our campus is cool because it is intertwined with the city almost seamlessly. The people of Ann Arbor respect the school and the students, and **everyone here has so much energy**. The city is very intellectual in nature, and Ann Arbor residents are very intelligent and educated."

Q "Students here rarely leave campus. Michigan is not a school where people look for an excuse to get out of town. **Nearly everyone stays put** once they get here. UM is not like other schools—suitcase colleges—where people go home all the time."

Q "**We hate Michigan State**. Here's the thing, the closest major city that we have here is Detroit. Usually, when you're at college near a major city, the thing to do is to go into the city to have a good time. Not here. Nobody really goes into Detroit. There's plenty to do here. People do go to Windsor, Ontario. Canada is supposed to be a good time because you can get into the casinos at 18 or 19, and the legal drinking age is 19. I've never been there, but I've heard nothing but good things about it."

The College Prowler Take On...
Local Atmosphere

Michigan students are quite content with their surroundings. Ann Arbor is a college town to the core, and you don't have to look hard to notice. The University and the city intertwine like threads into a rope. Moreover, it's hard to determine where the University ends and where the city begins—they are virtually one. There is always something to do, and students don't have to leave town for a good time.

Ann Arbor is the quintessential college town. It is safe, charming, picturesque, and friendly. For a city the size of Ann Arbor (well under 200,000), it is amazingly cosmopolitan. Ann Arbor has been touted as the arts center of Michigan, and you don't have to look far to realize it. On top of various cultural opportunities, there are great clubs, bars, coffeehouses, and local bookstores. Go shopping on State Street and Main Street, or enjoy a sunny day at the Arb (a huge arboretum). For a smaller city, the shopping is great. One of the original Urban Outfitters is right on campus, as are various trendy boutiques for the inner-sorority girl in you. The town has done well to steer clear of the rampant commercialism that has made towns across the country mirror images of one another. There are still used record shops, local coffee shops, and businesses as old as the University itself. Of course, Starbucks is making a presence, but not without student boycotts.

The College Prowler® Grade on

Local Atmosphere: B+

A high Local Atmosphere grade indicates that the area surrounding campus is safe and scenic. Other factors include nearby attractions, proximity to other schools, and the town's attitude toward students

Safety & Security

The Lowdown On...
Safety & Security

Number of UM Police:
60

UM Police Phone:
(734) 763-1131

Safety Services:
Night Owl Bus Service
Night Ride (taxi)
S.A.F.E.WALK

Health Services:
UHS (University Health Service) offers all basic medical services including STD screening

CAPS (Counseling and Psychological Services)

Health Center Office Hours:
8 a.m.-6 p.m.

"**Security at UM is excellent. Ann Arbor is only at about 40 percent of the national crime average. So, basically, you can walk around town at 4 a.m. and not have to worry about your safety.**"

"**I have never really felt unsafe** at UM. It's a big school, but the main campus is pretty compressed. At night, it's not the best idea to walk alone, but that is the case at most any campus. I think it is general knowledge that you shouldn't put yourself in a vulnerable situation. Overall, though, I feel safe."

"All of the residence halls have **secured entrances**. To get in, you have to swipe your M-Card, so people who don't belong there can't get in. I've never felt threatened on campus, even at night."

"I would not recommend visiting the University Health Service (UHS) for treatment **under any circumstances**. Let's just say they tend to misdiagnose."

"There are always Ann Arbor Police Officers around the campus and patrolling the streets. It makes you feel safe. Many of the cops are on mountain bikes, **just like Pacific Blue, only in Ann Arbor**. The whole city is very safe."

"I've always felt safe on campus, but lately there's been **some peeping Toms** in and around some of the dorms. I've never had this problem, nor do I know anyone who has, but it's been in the school paper. What can I say, some people are sickos."

Q "The University Health Service **isn't helpful at all**. You could walk in with pink-eye and be diagnosed with herpes!"

Q "I have never felt unsafe on campus. Like all campuses, there are dorm break-ins, drunks, freshmen, and so forth. However, I have never felt uncomfortable walking alone at night. There are a lot of safety options here (night walking systems, cabs, emergency phones, and well-lit areas). Safety is **not something I think or worry about**."

Q "Safety has a lot to do with where you choose to live. Most University housing is **within close walking distance** of the campus, bars, and libraries, and it is well lit. There are normally people out at all times of the day and night. Living off campus is a little different. The University provides free transportation to many areas, however a lot of times it is easier and faster to walk."

Q "Security here is generally good, but there are some break-ins at the dorms once in awhile. **Two people got shot at a house party**, but overall, it's pretty safe."

Q "The University **takes many precautions** to make sure that facilities are secured from all the criminals and rejects out there. Also, the campus is very well lit."

Q "Security on campus is good. There are security cars on campus, and there are such services as S.A.F.E.WALK, where students (usually one guy and one girl each trip) will walk with you if you want to be **accompanied home when it's late** and you're at the library or something."

Q "They claim that the security is good at UM, but we had **five break-ins into student dorms** and numerous reports of peeping Toms in the women's dorm bathrooms."

Q "There are **blue phones all around** campus that signal the police and flash a blue light if picked up."

Q "Security is good here, I suppose. There are lots of programs set up by the University to keep students safe. For example, the dorms can only be accessed with a student ID after 8 p.m. There is also **S.A.F.E.WALK**, which is a program set up for students who need someone to walk them home from the library after pulling a near all-nighter. I've personally never used it, but some of my female friends think it's great. Campus is also very well lit at night!"

Q "This year, there were some issues regarding security and safety here. I've been here for four years, and in the first three, there were no problems. But because of a few peeping Toms and some robberies, (which could have been avoided if people would lock their doors), security on campus **has been beefed up**, so it's pretty good now."

Q "The UM campus always felt pretty secure to me. **It is well lit** and everything. There are services such as the Night Owl bus service and Nite Ride that provide transportation from the library when it's late. On any University campus, you've got to be a little careful."

The College Prowler Take On...
Safety & Security

Since Ann Arbor is a relatively small city, most Michigan students feel relatively safe. There are few worries of major crime, and despite a few robberies and peeping Toms, students feel pretty secure in their college town. As of late, security has been beefed up, so most worries have subsided. If you want riots, tear gas, and burning couches, then feel free to head to Michigan State.

The University has its own police force, and when teamed with the AAPD, one needs to look no further for assistance. Sure, there are cases of petty theft, but Ann Arbor is a safe city with a highly-visible police force. Reviews of UHS (University Health Service) aren't so hot, although it's a free, comprehensive health service available to all University of Michigan students. Upon entry of the health center though, just be prepared to hear, "It's a virus." If you are seeking their advice, do yourself a favor and go someplace else! If you have a problem more serious than a cold or the flu, don't hesitate to venture to the University of Michigan Medical Center, which is among the top 10 hospitals in the nation. Overall, safety on campus isn't much of a worry to Michigan students, although someone may be watching you . . . just kidding.

B

The College Prowler® Grade on

Safety & Security: B

A high grade in Safety & Security means that students generally feel safe, campus police are visible, blue light phones and escort services are readily available, and safety precautions are not overly necessary.

Computers

The Lowdown On...
Computers

High-Speed Network?
Yes

Wireless Network?
Yes

Number of Labs:
14, plus a lab in every
residence hall

Operating Systems:
PC, MAC, UNIX

Number of Computers:
2,600

Free Software:
There's a "Blue Disk" that has
every software program
necessary at Michigan.

24-Hour Labs:
Angell Hall, Media Union

Charge to Print?
Free (with a 400-page limit
per semester)

Did You Know?

Angell Hall's computer lab, **the "Fishbowl,"** has over 400 workstations and is one of the largest collegiate computer labs in the country.

Each residence hall has its own computer lab **stocked with both PCs and Macs**.

Students Speak Out On...
Computers

{ **"I would recommend having your own computer, but all the dorms have computer labs, and so do all the libraries. There is no shortage of PCs and Macs on campus."**

Q "Computer labs are highly accessible and numerous at UM. They **all have T3 lines**, and the only time that they are crowded is around finals. During these times, you just have to find the labs that not many people know about, or just bring your own computer."

Q "I'd suggest **bringing your own computer**. I just find it to be more convenient. But the labs are not usually crowded except during mid-terms and finals—then you'll find yourself waiting around for a computer."

Q "**The Fishbowl rocks**. It's the best place to pull an all-nighter."

Q "The computer labs are good, but they can be crowded around finals time. If you need to do a lot of computer work for your major, bring one. Otherwise, **the school computers are fine**."

Q "Your own computer would be a plus for convenience sake. There are computer labs in every residence hall, and there are many other computer labs all over campus. I have my own computer, but it would have been **just as easy to use the school's**."

Q "I own a laptop, but I usually work in the Fishbowl. The computers are great, and the staff is **always willing to help you out**. I just like being around my peers when I work. As long as they're quiet, of course!"

Q "The computers in the labs are great. Computers are usually replaced or fully updated every year, and most of them have **flat-screen monitors**."

Q "If you have your own computer, you might want to bring it just for late nights, downloading, and whatnot. But there are tons of computers on campus; **you shouldn't have a big problem finding one**."

Q "I would strongly recommend bringing your own computer for the main reason that many **classes are becoming completely electronic**, meaning laptops are used to take class notes, access, and submit all assignments, and e-mail is the main communication between other students and professors. Group work is also becoming more prevalent in many departments. Meetings become much more productive and efficient when the majority of members are able to bring along laptops and work real time."

Q "**Ethernet rocks**! There are lots of computer labs, one in each dorm. Definitely bring your own computer if possible, though."

Q "I wouldn't have survived college at UM without a computer. There are computer labs everywhere, but the most convenient ones seem to be full, and who wants to wait around? **The network seems to work fine**, although, ironically, the engineering network seems to break down far more often than it should."

Q "If you can afford it, bring your own computer. The labs get **crowded during finals**, but you can usually find one. The network is good and has just been upgraded to one of the best in the country."

Q "I brought my own, but every dorm has a computer lab that's open 24 hours. It really is not a necessity, most of my friends do not have a computer, and they do just fine. I mean, **there are so many labs**, and most are either open 24 hours or stay open pretty late."

Q "Bring your own computer. Almost everyone does, and it is so much easier than using the computer labs. But there are always a few computers open. The Internet is T3, which is nice, and you have **plenty of storage space** and paper to use."

The College Prowler Take On...
Computers

Public universities may have their problems, but they also have huge upsides. One of those perks is the massive budget they usually command. This is why Michigan has plenty of computer facilities for the students to use, and most people agree that the computers and labs here are easily accessible, except during finals. Also, with technology this great, who would ever want to leave? Some people gripe about the wait during midterms and finals, but it's usually not that bad. But don't worry; if you get your work done ahead of time, then you won't be caught up in the finals rush anyway.

The computer facilities are great, but most students still recommend bringing your own computer. But with so many labs, including labs in each residence hall, one can easily get by without a computer. During peak periods, you may have to wait a few minutes for a computer, but in labs as large as the Fishbowl, you'll usually be hard at work (or playing solitaire) in no time. Also, in addition to Ethernet hookups in all dorms and many classrooms, more and more of the campus is connected to the wireless Web, which can be great for those long nights of studying in the library.

A

The College Prowler® Grade on
Computers: A

A high grade in Computers designates that computer labs are available, the computer network is easily accessible, and the campus' computing technology is up to date.

Facilities

The Lowdown On...
Facilities

Student Center:
The Michigan Union ("The Union") is the hub of all student activities. In addition to various restaurants and eateries, there are study areas, many meeting rooms and halls, a computer lab, a billiards room, psychological services, the Office of Greek life, and office space for hundreds of student organizations.

Libraries:
24, holding over 7.5 million volumes

Athletic Center:
CCRB (Central Campus Recreation Building)

NCRB (North Campus Recreation Building)

IM Building

Sports Coliseum

Campus Size:
3,070 acres

Popular Places to Chill:
The Diag

The Union

The Arb

What Is There to Do On Campus?

Michigan students have it all at their fingertips. From great restaurants in the Union, to nuclear testing labs, everything you'd ever want is on campus.

Movie Theatre on Campus?

Yes, Michigan Theatre

Bar on Campus?

No University-owned bars, but there are about 10 bars within five minutes of central campus.

Coffeehouse on Campus?

Yes, Cava Java, located in the Union

Favorite Things to Do

If it's a nice day, join thousands of fellow students on the Diag to bask in the sun or just hang out. Catch an independent movie at the Michigan Theatre, see a musical staged by the prestigious musical theater department at the Power Center, hear a concert at acoustically-perfect Hill Auditorium, or take a stroll in the Arboretum— the University's expansive park of rolling hills, running trails, and riverbeds.

> **"The Campus facilities are top-notch in my book. There is always a library open for you to study in if you need to get away from your room."**

"**The gyms here are good**. I work out on campus. The computer labs are good, although I really don't use them. The student center is really there to help with anything you need."

"Michigan has an amazing mix of **buildings, both old and new**. With all of the construction and renovation on campus, our facilities get better everyday. The technology and resources available on campus are second to none."

"There is **a lot of everything** at UM. On central campus, there are two gymnasium facilities owned by the school that are nice. I think there may be some privately-owned gyms and fitness clubs in the city, as well."

"The law quad is probably the most beautiful part of campus. It's like walking through **a gothic courtyard**. But, if you study in the Law Library's reading room, be quiet, because you can hear a pin drop! If you do happen to drop a pin, the law students might get annoyed and sue you in the near future."

Q "The library system here is incredible. Michigan's libraries are among the largest in the world, and **the collections are amazing**. If you need something, you'll find it. It just might take you some time."

Q "Overall, I would rate the facilities on campus as above average. There are some facilities on campus that are in **desperate need of an upgrade**. For example, the athletic facilities are a little shoddy, but even the outdated facilities provide adequate resources. Many of the facilities are state-of-the-art. The student centers and computer areas usually have the latest technology. The Business School recently opened a Financial Research and Trading Center that provides students with invaluable knowledge and instruction on research tools, and even simulates different trading experiences."

Q "**Angell Hall is so beautiful** and very stately. When taking a campus tour, it's a must see."

Q "Overall, the University recognizes the **need for continuous improvements** throughout the campus. However, more emphasis could be placed on extracurricular student needs, such as athletic facilities and student lounges."

Q "The facilities here are better than at many other midwestern universities. There are two main athletic complexes for students to use, so that's not a problem. The student center (we call it the 'Union') is large, and it's also a pretty famous building. The Union has a bunch of food places, a bookstore, pool hall, libraries, coffee shop, and much more. Overall, **I'm really satisfied**."

Q "The research facilities on North Campus are absolutely incredible. They have to be seen to be believed. **Wind tunnels, nuclear testing labs, audiovisual centers**, you name it, we got it."

Q "The facilities are great here. A lot of the classroom buildings are very historic with **ivy, wood, and the whole nine yards**. Other buildings are state-of-the-art brand spankin' new. Overall, UM provides its students with a very distinct learning environment."

The College Prowler Take On...
Facilities

The University of Michigan's facilities are outstanding. Although it has its fair share of older, historic buildings, they are all completely updated and well cared for. The newer buildings are simply amazing, and any school in the nation would be hard pressed to compete with the resources made available to Michigan students.

The University of Michigan seems to never rest when it comes to updating and building new facilities. Besides some outdated residence halls and older buildings here and there, most facilities are newly redone and up-to-date. Constant renovations on campus can be a bit irritating to students at UM, but they must realize that not everything can get done in the summer months. New buildings are popping up on campus all the time (the Life Sciences Institute, a new hulking three-building complex, right near central campus, was constructed just a few years ago), and while the vast majority of the buildings are aged and historic, their insides are fairly new. Some areas, such as library reading rooms, have retained their historic aura, as well. The gyms could be updated, and probably will be within the next few years, but from the stately law quad, to the NASA-sponsored research facilities on North Campus, the University of Michigan's facilities are very tough to beat.

A-

The College Prowler® Grade on

Facilities: A-

A high Facilities grade indicates that the campus is aesthetically pleasing and well maintained, facilities are state-of-the-art, and libraries are exceptional. Other determining factors include the quality of both athletic and student centers and an abundance of things to do on campus.

Campus Dining

The Lowdown On...
Campus Dining

Freshman Meal Plan Requirement?
Yes

Meal Plan Average Cost:
$2530

Places to Grab a Bite with Your Meal Plan:

Alice Lloyd Hall
Food: Cafeteria-style
Location: Hill area
Favorite dish: Quarter-pound hamburgers
Hours: Lunch Monday-Friday 11 a.m.-2 p.m.
Dinner Monday-Thursday 5 p.m.-7 p.m.

Betsy Barbour House

Food: Cafeteria-style

Location: Central Campus

Favorite dish: Lemon pepper chicken breast

Hours: Lunch Monday-Friday 11 a.m.-2 p.m., Dinner Monday-Thursday 4:30 p.m.-7 p.m.

Bursley Hall

Food: Cafeteria-style

Location: North Campus

Favorite dish: Baked chicken

Hours: Breakfast Monday-Friday 7 a.m.- 10 a.m.

Lunch Sunday 10 a.m.-2:30 p.m. Monday-Friday 10:30 a.m.-3 p.m., Saturday 11 a.m.- 2 p.m., Dinner Sunday-Friday 4 p.m.-7:30 p.m.

Couzens Hall

Food: Cafeteria-style

Location: Hill area

Favorite dish: Hawaiian chicken

Hours: Lunch Sunday-Friday 11 a.m.- 2 p.m., Dinner Monday-Friday 4:30 p.m.-7 p.m.

Mary Markley Hall

Food: Cafeteria-style

Location: Hill area

Favorite dish: Bowtie pasta bandiera

Hours: Breakfast Monday Friday 7:30 a.m.- 9:45 a.m., Lunch Sunday 10:30 a.m.-2:15 p.m., Monday-Friday 10:30 a.m.- 3:15 p.m., Saturday 11 a.m.-2:15 p.m.. Dinner Sunday-Friday 4 p.m.-7:45 p.m.

Mosher-Jordan Hall

Food: Cafeteria-style

Location: Hill area

Favorite Dish: Cheese lasagna rollups

Hours: Lunch Monday-Friday 11 a.m.-2 p.m., Dinner Monday-Thursday 4:30 p.m.-7 p.m.

Stockwell Hall

Food: Cafeteria-style

Location: Hill area

Favorite dish: Chicken patty parmesan

Hours: Breakfast Monday Friday 7:30 a.m.- 10 a.m., Lunch Sunday-Friday 10:30 a.m.-2 p.m., Saturday 11 a.m.-2 p.m., Dinner Sunday-Friday 4:30 p.m.- 7:30 p.m.

Campus Restaurants

Alice's Place

Food: "Grab and go" snacks

Location: The first floor of Alice Lloyd Hall

Favorite dish: Breakfast sandwiches

Hours: Monday-Friday 7:30 a.m.-10 p.m., Saturday 12 p.m.-9 p.m., Sunday closed

Café ConXion

Food: Smoothies, Starbucks coffee, pastries, and deli sandwiches

Location: Just to the right of the entrance to the South Quad dining hall.

Favorite Dish: Strawberry smoothies

Hours: Monday-Thursday 7:30 a.m.-12 a.m., Friday-Saturday 9 a.m.-10 p.m. Sunday closed

East Quadrangle Halfway Inn

Food: Deli sanwiches, vegetarian entrees, various grilled items

Location: East Quadrangle

Favorite Dish: Grilled chicken

Hours: Monday-Thursday 12 p.m.-11 p.m. Friday-Saturday 12 p.m.-9 p.m Sunday closed

24-Hour On-Campus Eating?

No

Student Favorites:

Bursley and Markley Residence Halls

Did You Know?

Your M-Card (student ID card) has a feature called **"Entrée Plus"** which can store money for use in many restaurants within campus buildings, including those listed on the previous pages.

If you miss the normal meal hours, grab a bite in East Quad's **"Halfway Inn."** Your meal plan works there just as it does in the cafeterias.

Students Speak Out On...
Campus Dining

"Dorm food here isn't bad. I think the best dorm overall is Couzens, but the best dorm food is at Bursley."

Q "Dorm food is dorm food, and it's no different here. East Quad is notorious for a lot of vegetarian dishes. There are kosher meals somewhere on campus. West Quad and South Quad have great dining, and most dorms have some sort of after-hours café. West Quad is also attached to the Union, where you can buy things like Wendy's, First Wok, and pizza by using money on your M-Card."

Q "I feel that, compared to other schools, Michigan's food can't really compete. It's pretty much just the basics here. There are no extra frills or specialty foods available."

Q "The food here is quite good. The best dorm food is in Bursley; the second best is in South Quad."

Q "I live in Betsey Barbour, which has the best food on campus! I'm lucky. Some food places really suck, but there are enough good places around to balance it out (South Quad, Betsey Barbour, and Mary Markley, to name a few)."

Q "The campus dining halls are scary. Avoid them especially at the end of the week—the week's leftovers are combined to make new treats."

Q "Make sure to **get Entrée Plus**. It's so convenient. Although few students have meal plans after freshman year, many have Entrée Plus, so they can eat 'for free' in the Union, or other places around campus."

Q "Lesson one in higher education is that all college food sucks. It's all bad, but the best spot on North campus is Bursley. On Central, it's South Quad, and on the Hill, it's Markley Hall. But as I said, all college campus food is horrible. **UM is no exception**."

Q "**Make your own waffles** and get an omelet however you like it at Sunday brunch. That's the best food here."

Q "Dorm food isn't too bad at UM. The food at Bursley is the best if you ask me. Also, if you get a meal plan, then you can eat at **Wendy's, Tim Horton's, McDonald's** and other places—just like eating a meal in the dorm!"

Q "The campus food is okay. **Dorm food is pretty consistent** across campus, but people say that Bursley Hall has the best food. I stayed there freshman year, and I think that the only reason Bursley is the 'best' is because it has the most options at all times."

Q "The food at the dining halls might not be the best around, but **they offer much more than food**. They are a place to meet people, take a break from the studying, and just hang out with friends. And what the dining halls lack in quality and variety, the city of Ann Arbor more than makes up for. There are so many fantastic restaurants that living there for four years is not even close to enough time to try them all. There are also so many places and traditions that are unique to Ann Arbor. Frozen yogurt colliders at Rod's, pizza sticks at Charley's, and chipatis at Pizza House are only familiar to Michigan students and alumni."

Q "Go to Bursley and get served by '**Sexy Grandpa**.' He knows everyone's name, and has worked there for decades. He is a campus legend!"

Q "There are plenty of good places to eat on campus; it's just that most of them are not in the dorms. Mr. Spots is a very good spot for hoagies and Philly cheesesteaks, and Pizza House is a good all-around food joint. China Chef probably has **the best Chinese food on campus**, and Jimmy John's is great for a late-night sandwich."

Q "The dorm food is okay. Stockwell, Barbour, and Bursley Halls have the better cafeterias. If you are going to live in the dorms, you will get to eat at any of them, **regardless of where you stay**."

The College Prowler Take On...
Campus Dining

Surprisingly, the majority of student comments about the campus food at UM aren't entirely pessimistic. Everyone admits it's not the best food, but it seems to get fewer complaints than some schools. The student body overwhelmingly picks North Campus's Bursley Hall as the dorm with the best food service, and East Quad gets the lowest marks, so bear that in mind if you choose Michigan.

The dorms offer several dining choices and generally seem to do the most they can with what they have, which would explain the funny-looking meatloaf at the end of the week. As compared to other schools with improved dining options, Michigan offers the typical: hot and cold entrees, a salad bar, and desserts. Weekend brunches are known by many students as the best cooked meals of the week, and don't be surprised to see tired and hungover classmates wearing pajamas and slippers. For what it's worth, you can get by just fine, but don't expect to write home about how great the grub is.

The College Prowler® Grade on

Campus Dining: C+

Our grade on Campus Dining addresses the quality of both school-owned dining halls and independent on campus restaurants as well as the price, availability, and variety of food available.

Off-Campus Dining

The Lowdown On...
Off-Campus Dining

Restaurant Prowler:
Popular Places to Eat!

Angelo's
Food: Diner, breakfast

1100 Catherine Street

Cool Features: Best breakfast in town. Be prepared to wait in line.

Price: $9-12 a person

Hours: Monday-Friday 6 a.m.-3 p.m., Saturday 6 a.m.-3 p.m., Sunday 7 a.m.-2 p.m.

BD's Mongolian Barbeque
Food: Barbecue, stir-fry

200 S. Main Street

Cool Features: Make your own stir-fry, and they cook it on a big grill in the center of the restaurant. Fun atmosphere, and always very crowded.

Price: $15 a person

Hours: Monday-Friday 11 a.m.-11 p.m., Saturday 10 a.m.-2 a.m., Sunday 1 p.m.-10 p.m.

Champion House

Food: Chinese

120 E Liberty Street

Cool Features: Chinese on one side, a Japanese steak house on the other.

Price: $10 and over a person

Hours: Monday-Thursday 11 a.m.-10:30 p.m., Friday-Saturday 11 a.m.-11 p.m., Sunday 12 p.m.-9:30 p.m.

China Gate

Food: Chinese

1201 S University Avenue

Cool Features: With only about 15 tables, this cozy take-out or sit-and-eat place serves all your favorites at low prices and at speeds only the UM astrophysists can measure.

Price: $5 and over a person

Hours: Daily 11 a.m.-10 p.m.

Cottage Inn

Food: Pizza

1141 Broadway Street

Cool Features: Has been open since 1948

Price: $5 and over

Hours: Open 24 hours

The Earle

Food: French and Italian

121 W Washington Street

Cool Features: Live music.

Price: $15-$20 a person

Hours: Open Monday-Thursday 5:30 p.m.-10 p.m. Friday 5:30 p.m.-12 a.m., Sat 6 p.m.-12 a.m., Sun 5 p.m.-9 p.m.

Good Time Charley's

Food: American

1140 South University

Cool Features: Great happy hour specials every night, very popular with students.

Price: $7-10 a person

Hours: Monday-Saturday 11 a.m.-2 a.m., Sunday 12 p.m.-12 a.m.

The Gandy Dancer

Food: Seafood

401 Depot Street

Cool Features: Made out of a converted train station.

Price: $15 and over a person

Hours:
Lunch: Monday - Friday 11:30 a.m.-3:30 a.m.

Dinner: Monday-Thursday 4:30 p.m.-10 p.m., Friday-Saturday 4:30-11 p.m. Sunday 3:30 p.m.-9 p.m.

Brunch: Sunday 10 a.m.-2 p.m.

Gratzi

Food: Italian

326 South Main Street

Cool Features: Sit upstairs at a table in the window.

Price: $15-20 a person

Hours: Monday-Thursday 11:30 a.m.-10 p.m., Friday-Saturday 11:30 a.m.-11 p.m., Sunday 4 p.m.-9 p.m.

Jimmy John's

Food: Sub sandwiches

Many locations

Cool Features: Cheap subs that taste great. You'll learn to love them!

Price: Under $5 a person

Hours: Vary for each location

Maize N Blue Deli

Food: Deli sandwiches

1329 S. University

Cool Features: The sandwiches are so big, order a half and you'll be fine.

Price: $7-10 a person

Hours: Monday-Saturday 11 a.m.-2 a.m., Sunday 12 p.m.-12 a.m.

Mr. Greek's Coney Island

Food: Greek, diner-style

215 South State Street

Cool Features: A great place to grab a late breakfast.

Price: $7-10 a person

Hours: Weekdays 11 a.m.-9 p.m., Saturday-Sunday 12 p.m.-12 a.m.

Palio

Food: Italian

347 South Main Street

Cool Features: Dine on the roof in the summer.

Price: $10-15 a person

Hours: Monday-Thursday 5 p.m.-9:30 p.m., Friday-Saturday 5 p.m.-10:30 p.m., Sunday 4 p.m.-8:30 p.m.

Pizza House

Food: Pizza

618 Church Street

Cool Features: Over 40 delivery drivers on the payroll.

Price: $5-$7 a person

Hours: Open daily 10:30 a.m.-4 p.m.

Red Hawk Bar & Grill

Food: American

316 South State Street

Cool Features: Great burgers and many beers on tap.

Price: $10-15 a person

Hours: Monday-Saturday 11 a.m.-2 a.m., Sunday 12 p.m.-12 a.m.

Rod's Diner

Food: American diner-style, ice-cream treats, colliders!

812 South State Street

Cool Features: Collider, which is like a flurry, but much better.

Price: $5

Hours: Monday-Saturday 3 p.m.-9 p.m., Sunday 1 p.m.-5 p.m.

Sweetwater's Cafe

Food: Coffee, pastries

123 W. Washington St.

Cool Features: Is also a sweet nightspot

Price: $5-$10 per person

Hours: Monday-Friday 7 a.m.-12 a.m. Saturday 8 a.m.-12 a.m., Sunday 8:30 a.m.-11 p.m.

Zingerman's Deli

Food: Deli sandwiches

422 Detroit St

Cool Features: One of the most popular delis in Ann Arbor.

Price: $5-10 a person

Hours: Monday-Sunday 7 a.m.-10 p.m.

24-Hour Eating:
Fleetwood Diner

Best Pizza:
Gratzi

Best Chinese:
Champion House

Best Breakfast:
Angelo's

Best Wings:
BD's Mongolian BBQ

Best Healthy:
Red Hawk

Best Place to Take Your Parents:
Gratzi or The Gandy Dancer

Student Favorites:
BD's Mongolian Barbeque

Good Time Charley's

Rod's Diner

Students Speak Out On...
Off-Campus Dining

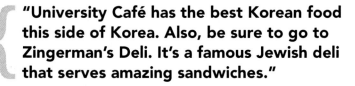

"University Café has the best Korean food this side of Korea. Also, be sure to go to Zingerman's Deli. It's a famous Jewish deli that serves amazing sandwiches."

Q "Ann Arbor has some of the best restaurants in the state of Michigan—not that that's saying much! Ann Arbor has restaurants for everyone, from very elegant places such as Gratzi or The Gandy Dancer, to places like **Mongolian BBQ**, which is a great place to go for lunch or dinner. Everything is relatively close, too."

Q "Pizza House is the best place for eating out in Ann Arbor. It has great pizzas, ruben sandwiches, and baked pasta. They are open and **deliver until 3 a.m.** There are just so many great places to eat in Ann Arbor! And they are right on-campus. There's Champion House, Good Time Charley's, Cottage Inn, and many more."

Q "Ann Arbor has a ton of great places to eat. Ann Arbor has everything from the cheaper, **'broke college kid' places**, to upper class dining where you can take your parents, all within walking distance. Popular places to eat around campus are Champion House and Good Time Charley's. There are many places that deliver, as well."

Q "The best restaurants are on Main Street, but they're a bit out of the way and expensive. The South University strip feels like a classic college town and has plenty of options for whatever you crave. Zingerman's Deli is off campus, but **it's world-famous** and worth the trip."

Q "There's always fast food available at U of M. The pizza places are really good (they have way more than pizza) and they deliver until 4 a.m., but **some of them are pretty expensive**. Mongolian BBQ is also good, it's downtown and also quite expensive."

Q "Rod's Diner has the best snacks. **Get a collider**, which is basically a flurry, but 10 times better. You can put as many toppings on as you want, from cereal to fresh fruit."

Q "Ann Arbor has so many restaurants—it's hard to separate them all. **All eateries are within walking distance**. My personal late night snack place is across the street at The Red Hawk, which is on South State Street."

Q "Off-campus restaurants are abundant and delicious. Although there is not really a need to go anyway because there are so many great places on campus, leaving campus for a few hours is always **a great little escape**. Main Street boasts a variety of wonderful restaurants, from the romantic atmosphere of Gratzi to the always crowded Mongolian BBQ, to the trendy sushi place Wasabi. With over 300 restaurants, there really is a place for any taste you might have."

Q "There are many places open late night, within walking distance, and with **ethnic variety**. Everything is quality, and lots of places deliver. You won't go hungry! "

Q "The **local coffee shops are great**. Check out Sweetwater's and Zola around the Main Street area."

Q "Make sure to check out **Panchero's Mexican food**, as well as Champion House for Chinese or Saigon Garden for good Vietnamese food."

Q "For delivery at economic prices, Jimmy John's and Mr. Greek's is what I lived off of. The food in Ann Arbor is incredible; it has **more restaurants than it does people**, and there's food from all over the world. If you have the money or want to treat yourself once in a while, I really enjoyed Mongolian BBQ and Champion House and too many more to list."

Q "The campus is right in the middle of the city, so there are many restaurants to choose from, whether you want pizza or something fancy. **Gratzi is the ideal restaurant** to take a date."

The College Prowler Take On...
Off-Campus Dining

Although your meal plan may suffice, no one can resist the temptation of eating at any of the large variety of off-campus restaurants, most of which are as close to campus, if not closer, than the dorms themselves. If it's late-night food you're craving, hit up Jimmy John's, Panchero's, or Backroom Pizza. NYPD Pizza is well liked by students, too, but be prepared for a wait. All in all, the off-campus eats are great in Ann Arbor, and few students complain about the lack of options.

So many restaurants, so little time! For a smaller town, Ann Arbor offers a selection of restaurants that's hard to believe. You could eat out every night of the week, and have a hard time eating at the same place twice. There is a selection of nearly every ethnic cuisine under the sun, as well as some great American comfort food. From late-night burritos at Panchero's, to Ethiopian food at the Blue Nile, and everything in between, Ann Arbor's got it all and, oh yeah, the food tastes good, too.

The College Prowler® Grade on
Off-Campus Dining: B+

A high off campus dining grade implies that off campus restaurants are affordable, accessible, and worth visiting. Other factors include the variety of cuisine and the availability of alternative options (vegetarian, vegan, kosher, etc.).

Campus Housing

The Lowdown On...
Campus Housing

Room Types:
Single, Double, Triple

Best Dorms:
Markley
South Quad

Worst Dorm:
Fletcher

Undergrads on Campus:
37%

Number of Dormitories:
16 (13 available to freshman)

Number of University-owned Apartments:
17

Dormitories:

Alice Lloyd
Floors: 5
Number of Occupants: 500
Bathrooms: Community
Coed: Yes
Room Types: Double
Special Features: 68% Lloyd Hall Scholars Program

Baits I & II Houses
Floors: 3
Number of Occupants: 830
Bathrooms: Community
Coed: Yes
Rooms Types: Single, Double
Special Features: Mostly non-freshmen

Betsey Barbour House
Floors: 4
Number of Occupants: 120
Bathrooms: Community
Coed: No, all female
Room Types: Single, Double

Bursley
Floors: 4
Number of Occupants: 1,240
Bathrooms: Community
Coed: Yes
Room Types: Single, Double

Couzens
Floors: 5
Number of Occupants: 570
Bathrooms: Community
Coed: Yes
Room Types: Single, Double, Triple
Special Features: 35% Michigan Community Scholars Program

East Quadrangle
Floors: 4
Number of Occupants: 830
Bathrooms: Community
Coed: Yes.
Room Types: Single, Double, Triple
Special Features: 57% Residential College, many non-freshmen

Fletcher Hall
Floors: 3
Number of Occupants: 75
Bathrooms: Community
Coed: Yes
Room Types: Double
Special Features: Community kitchen, many non-freshmen

Helen Newberry House

Floors: 4

Number of Occupants: 110

Bathrooms: Community

Coed: No, all female

Room Types: Single, Double, Triple

Mosher-jordan

Floors: 5

Number of Occupants: 175

Bathrooms: Community

Coed: Yes

Room Types: Single, Double, Triple

Special Features: 24% Women in Science and Engineering; 28% UROP

South Quad

Floors: 8

Number of Occupants:1,220

Bathrooms: Community

Coed: Yes.

Room Types: Single, Double, Triple

Special Features: Many athletes

Stockwell

Floors: 5

Number of Occupants: 400

Bathrooms: Community

Coed: No, all female

Room Types: Single, Double, Triple

West Quad

Floors: 5

Number of Occupants: 1,000

Bathrooms: Community

Coed: Yes

Room Types: Single, Double, Triple

Special Features: Some rooms have sinks, many non-freshman

Did You Know?

Each residence hall is separated into "Houses," which basically amounts to a certain wing of the residence hall itself, often including both men and women. Residents can get involved with their respective house councils, and there are intramurals within each house that compete against other houses and organizations across campus. **House activities are a great way to meet new people**.

What You Get

Dormitories
Each student receives a bed, desk, chair, bookshelf, closet, dresser, window coverings, cable TV jack, Ethernet connection, phone line, and mirror.

Apartments
Each student receives a bed, kitchen facilities, bathrooms, living area furnishings, desk chair, eating table and chairs, closet space, dresser, Ethernet port, and telephone with free local and campus phone calls.

Also Available

Substance-free housing, special-interest housing

Bed Type

Twin extra-long for all beds (39" x 80")

Available for Rent

Mini-fridge with microwave

{ **"Markley is definitely the most social dorm. Stockwell is pretty quiet and tame. South Quad is a lot of fun, too, and it's very close to campus."**

Q "The dorms are pretty good, overall. Unless you're an engineer or an art student of any kind, I'd **avoid Bursley and Baits like the plague**. They're on North Campus, and that's a 10-15 minute bus ride from Central Campus (where practically everything is). North Campus is like Canada: It's our friendly neighbor to the North. Most people never go up there unless they absolutely have to, or because they got stuck living there as freshmen."

Q "I think **Markley's rooms may be the smallest**, but who cares. West Quad's rooms are the biggest."

Q "Michigan hasn't built a new dorm in something like 40 years, and it definitely shows. **Don't expect anything modern or spacious**. Those interested in the Greek system will want to stay on the Hill, although it's inconvenient and loud. West Quad and South Quad are probably the nicest dorms, and they certainly have the best location. East Quad is known for having a lot of independent-minded residents, the artsy types. There is also Bursley on North Campus. Although Bursley supposedly has the best food on campus, you can kiss your social life goodbye."

Q "North Campus **isn't as bad as everyone says it is**. I've lived there for two years, and I have a blast!"

Q "I lived on West Quad freshman year. I had a sink in my room, and the room was huge. But I don't think it was as fun as the Hill dorms, because my hall was small, and there were **a lot of sophomores**."

Q "Some of the dorms here suck. Being on North Campus will suck altogether. But Bursley is actually a pretty nice dorm. I live in Betsey Barbour on Central campus and love it. West Quad and South Quad are in a **perfect location**, and it's a small dorm. Mary Markley is nice, but a little bit of a walk to classes."

Q "Bursley is on North Campus by the engineering school, a 10-minute bus ride from Central Campus. **I liked Stockwell**. Generally, the farther you are from Central Campus (where you want to be), the larger the room and the better the food. I guess it kind of balances out that way."

Q **"South Quad and Bursley are the best dorms available**. Pick those if you can."

Q "If I could do it all over, I would live on the Hill. It's more fun being there with **all of the freshmen**. Dorms on Central Campus seem to have more upperclassman."

Q "Living on the Hill is the best place to be. It's mostly freshmen, and you're surrounded by a lot of dorms. **Markley is really big but fun**, and Lloyd is what I recommend."

Q "There are three all-female dorms: Betsey Barbour, Helen Newberry, and Stockwell. Most **people call Stockwell the 'Virgin Vault,'** but I don't think that's the case."

Q "Dorms at UM are ok, but some suck. **You don't have a choice, though**. You go where they put you. Just hope to live on Central Campus."

Q "Well, you want to be on Central Campus, since that is where most of your classes will be unless you are in the school of music or engineering school. I lived in South Quad, and I liked it there because it was **so easy to get everywhere**."

The College Prowler Take On...
Campus Housing

Dorm life on the Michigan campus isn't really about being good or bad, comfortable or uncomfortable, fun or lame—it's just there. Almost every freshman lives in the dorms, and if some are better than others, it's just the luck of the draw. You can't pick your dorm, but you can request a specific area. Most recommend choosing either Central Campus or the Hill, and most choose North Campus last. Either way, students at UM live with what they get.

At a school the size of Michigan, the dorms vary greatly. Most people choose to live in them only for their freshman year. The highest concentration of freshmen is found on the Hill (Markley, Alice Lloyd, Couzens, MoJo, Stockwell) and in South Quad. Also, many are assigned to Bursley on North Campus. Many treat this like a death sentence but soon find themselves in a state of euphoria, as those living in this dorm are a tightly-knit bunch. Also, the food is said to be the best dorm food on campus. The most social dorms are thought to be Markley and South Quad. The dorms vary from absolutely beautiful and ivy-covered (Stockwell, MoJo, West Quad), to rather ugly, with that '50s barracks sort of feel (Markley). Either way, the rooms are quite similar, and rather bland—although some are larger than others, and some have amenities like sinks and larger closets. The dorms at U of M are nothing spectacular, but it doesn't seem to matter since the residents are what make all the fun.

The College Prowler® Grade on

Campus Housing: C+

A high Campus Housing grade indicates that dorms are clean, well-maintained and spacious. Other determining factors include variety of dorms, proximity to classes and social atmosphere.

Off-Campus Housing

The Lowdown On...
Off-Campus Housing

Undergrads in Off-Campus Housing:
63%

Average Rent For:
1BR Apt.: $700-800/month
2BR Apt.: $1100 per month
3BR Apt.: $1000+/month

Popular Areas:
Anywhere near campus—south of campus is the area with the most students, but anywhere in the area surrounding campus is occupied predominantly by students.

Best Time to Look For a Place:
Early fall

Students Speak Out On...
Off-Campus Housing

"You'll pay a lot, but living off campus is so fun, and it's certainly worth the added freedom and all."

"Housing off campus is okay. There are a lot of houses and apartments available—some good and some not so good. One negative aspect of Ann Arbor is that housing **prices are pretty steep**. U of M is actually one of the most expensive public universities in the nation—it blows at times, but you get used to it."

"Living off campus is not too bad. I've lived off campus for the last two years, and I haven't had any problems with it. The only thing is that **it is very competitive**—you've got to start looking early if you want to find someplace close and nice to live."

"Ann Arbor has tons of apartments and houses for rent all around campus. A large chunk of the student body live off-campus after freshman year, and almost everybody does after two years. Be sure to **look for places early**. It's not unusual for the nicer spots on campus to be rented by October the year before."

"Off-campus houses and apartments are **all close to campus**, and I would say that there is always someone looking for a roommate or housemate."

"A lot of houses are **pretty rundown**, but no one really seems to care."

Q "If you're a freshman, **live in the dorms**! Otherwise, housing is available, but it's kind of expensive."

Q "I loved my off-campus houses. It was so much fun living with five of my best friends. Also, most houses are **closer to campus than the dorms**, so that's nice."

Q "I lived off campus my last year with no car, and it was not that bad. **Most people move off** after their first or second year, so it is pretty convenient."

Q "I lived close to where the marching band practiced every morning. That definitely got old really quick. Be sure to check out the **conditions of housing** before committing."

Q "Off-campus housing is plentiful, but beware of the costs. **Rent in Ann Arbor is ridiculous**. The average price for a 1000 square foot, two-bedroom apartment is $1500/month. If you are an incoming freshman, I'd definitely recommend staying in the dorms at least for a year, if not more—that's where you make friends anyway."

Q "Housing is very **convenient but very expensive**. Student housing isn't the greatest on campus. The houses and apartments are pretty small, and some are run down. They charge an arm and a leg to live in them."

Q "Getting off-campus housing is insane here. People start looking for housing for the following year at the very beginning of fall semester, and **most people have signed leases by Thanksgiving**. It gets kind of competitive."

Q "Ann Arbor isn't traditional in the sense of on- versus off-campus housing options. The college students and the residents all **share one little city**. There is no clear-cut divide between on and off campus. There is limited space, and prime housing is extremely expensive."

The College Prowler Take On...
Off-Campus Housing

It's clear that students are pretty apathetic about dorm life on the University of Michigan campus, but off-campus housing is another story. Although it's a whole lot easier to live in the dorms and tolerate the lousy food, most students move off campus after their first year. Many gripe about the outlandish prices, but most enjoy their college digs and the freedom that comes with them.

Nearly everyone moves off campus for their second through fourth years. Everywhere is within walking distance, and the entire town is filled with students. Literally, there are blocks and blocks of houses and apartments in which there are nothing but students. There are really no apartment complexes to speak of, since most people live in whole houses with a bunch of friends, or in apartments within houses. It's difficult to describe the area, but picture an established neighborhood with tree-lined streets and sidewalks with nothing but houses full of students—wild and crazy students! At three in the morning on a weekend night you'll see tons of students just out and about. Off-campus living is something that makes the Michigan experience great. Some downsides: it's really expensive, most homes are older, and to find a great place for the next year, you need to start looking at the beginning of the semester.

B-

The College Prowler® Grade on

Off-Campus
Housing: B-

A high grade in Off-Campus Housing indicates that apartments are of high quality, close to campus, affordable, and easy to secure.

Diversity

The Lowdown On...
Diversity

Native American:
1%

White:
69%

Asian American:
12%

International:
5%

African American:
8%

Out-of-State:
34%

Hispanic American:
5%

Political Activity

Politics are a hot issue on campus, although most students lean towards the left. The University has long been a center of student protest, dating back to the civil rights era. Today, you'll still find your fair share of protests and rallies, but the campus is not as active as in the past.

Gay Pride

The University of Michigan community, for the most part, is very accepting of the gay community.

Economic Status

Although Michigan students come from diverse economic backgrounds, there seems to be a preponderance of students coming from very wealthy families.

Minority Clubs

Many minority clubs are quite visible and are well received on campus. Often, minority groups sponsor dances and parties that are open to the entire University community.

Most Popular Religions

Judaism, Christianity

Students Speak Out On...
Diversity

> "This campus is very diverse. There are people from every culture imaginable at U of M."

Q "It's moderately diverse here. There's certainly a **large white population**, but there are minorities on campus. The two largest minority groups here, I think, are blacks and Asians."

Q "The school is very diverse, but there is **a major East Coast feel** to the school. A lot of students have a lot of money, and they make it pretty obvious."

Q "We are an extremely diverse university. We have many organizations that cover about every minority you can imagine, and we have **a totally liberal atmosphere**."

Q "Michigan is extremely **well known for its diversity**, and this is one of my favorite aspects of the campus. Prior to attending the University, I did not know the richness that diversity can bring to your life. My experience at the business school was greatly enhanced by the many cultures and experiences that the diverse student body provided."

Q "**If you're a Republican, you're a minority** at Michigan."

Q "This is **one of the most diverse campuses** in the world. A really large number of different countries are represented here."

Q "The gay community is pretty active on campus and is **pretty well tolerated**."

Q "Diversity is a huge issue on campus, with the affirmative action lawsuits focusing the national diversity spotlight on Ann Arbor. There's a cultural group for every possible cultural identity, but the result is an unfortunate **self-segregation** that plagues much of campus. While the student population as a whole is diverse, people tend to group themselves with similar people."

Q "UM is definitely **the most diverse school in Michigan**. And I'd say, statistically, UM is one of the most diverse public schools in the nation."

Q "There is a **large Jewish population** on campus."

Q "Well, I am black, and there are a lot of **different racial groups on campus**, but diversity is what you make of it here. You can chose to take advantage of it or not, but it is there to do with as you please."

Q "It seems like Metro Detroit has the largest Arab population in the world (outside of the Middle East, of course). There was definitely some **tension on campus** post-9/11, but overall, I think Michigan students are open-minded and accepting of differences."

Q "We have a large population of **African Americans and Asians**; we're known to be one of the most diverse campuses across America. Affirmative action was a hot debate on campus, with our school being sued in the Supreme Court and all."

Q "I'm from New York City, and even compared to that, **I think that Michigan is incredibly diverse**. Although I came from a diverse city, my school wasn't very diverse, so it's great taking classes with such a diverse group of wonderful people."

The College Prowler Take On...
Diversity

Compared to most campuses, Michigan's is quite diverse in many ways. The school is known to be open-minded and liberal, so diversity is something that is prized here by students and faculty alike. Although you may often see racial groups as separate entities, their presence on campus seems to make a large impact, and students at Michigan definitely notice the many groups of people from different backgrounds on campus.

Simply stated, there are few schools more diverse than the University of Michigan. Socio-economically speaking, a large number of students come from a wealthy background, and you'll see plenty of BMWs and SUVs driving around campus, but many other backgrounds are visible on campus, as well. In addition to socio-economic and racial diversity, Michigan is very geographically diverse for a public school, and many out-of-state students come from the East Coast, Chicago, California, and Florida, as well as the surrounding Midwest. If you're not used to the East Coast mentality, you'll soon get used to it, which does seem a little odd since Michigan is far from the East Coast. Although the administration was under intense nationwide scrutiny regarding their admissions practices not too long ago, the diversity on campus is one thing that sets Michigan apart from other institutions. At Michigan, students seem to learn just as much outside of the classroom as they do inside, and that can be attributed to the multitude of races, opinions, and backgrounds of the students.

The College Prowler® Grade on

Diversity: B

A high grade in Diversity indicates that ethnic minorities and international students have a notable presence on campus, and that students of different economic backgrounds, religious beliefs, and sexual preferences are well-represented.

Guys & Girls

The Lowdown On...
Guys & Girls

Women Undergrads:	Men Undergrads:
51%	49%

Birth Control Available?
Yes, there are free condoms at UHS. UHS also prescribes birth control medications to females.

Social Scene
Like all colleges, the social scene at Michigan revolves around the weekend. Depending on your scene, most of the action happens at the bars, house parties, or frats, with the most hookups taking place at frat parties, although the bar brings its fair share of hookups.

Hookups or Relationships?

For the most part, serious relationships aren't all that common on Michigan's campus. The ongoing hookup is common, but relationships at UM never seem to advance much beyond that. Of course, there are people that have serious relationships, and people do couple off, but mostly, it's just big groups of friends going out together.

Best Place to Meet Guys/Girls

At Michigan, there is no best place to meet others, but some of the most obvious hotspots are frat parties, house parties, in class, and dorms. Yes, class was included in that list. In certain classes, especially those that are discussion-based, it's quite easy to turn on the charm and win someone over. It happens time and time again (just one more reason to pay attention in class). Of course, the Greek scene is like one large family where everyone seems to know everyone else, so you can always get set-up that way.

Another social atmosphere is the UGLi (Undergraduate Library). It sounds dorky, but this is one of the largest social centers on campus. People don't study at the UGLi because it's peaceful and quiet, they go to do group work, and often it's abuzz with chatter. You'll always see someone you know, and, if you're doing group work, it's the perfect place to work your "Don Juan" magic.

Did You Know?

Top Places to Find Hotties:
1. Frat parties
2. Class
3. Rick's

Students Speak Out On...
Guys & Girls

"There is no lack of eye candy here—whether you are male or female. The campus, overall, is pretty darn attractive."

Q "Whether you're looking for **Mr. Right or Mr. Right Now**, you'll find him at UM."

Q "Girls are definitely hot at U of M. When I first got here, things weren't quite as good, but there are definitely a lot of hot girls around campus now. The girls here are maybe a little **too hot for their own good** sometimes."

Q "The highest concentration of hot girls is in the Greek system. Some houses are **almost 100 percent blonde**, others are all beautiful dark-haired chicks. The spring is the
best time of year here. It's when all the hot girls come out from hibernation."

Q "Truthfully, this is a slightly above-average campus as far as attractiveness goes, but I think that's a result of being an academically competitive school. Schools like Michigan State have lots of hot girls, but **getting them to count to 10 is a different story**. However, there are some really attractive guys and really attractive girls if you're willing to look around for them."

Q "The **beautiful people** here make the nightlife that much better."

Q "I guess it depends on what you consider hot. Michigan is notorious for **not having any hot guys**, but it doesn't seem to be true when you look around."

Q "It depends what you're into. If you want **hot sorority chicks and sexy frat guys**, then you've got plenty to choose from at UM. But, on the other end of the spectrum, there is a large population of hippie types who could care less about how they appear to others. I guess that, overall, the students are pretty good looking here."

Q "It's hard to tell what the girls look like most of the year under three layers of North Face attire. It's always entertaining the first time it hits 60 degrees—you see what the girls really look like. Michigan's girls must be **tops in the Big Ten**, but it's no southern school, though."

Q "The girls here are so hot that I sometimes have a hard time **paying attention in class**."

Q "The guys here seem to **care about their appearance**, so there are plenty of hot guys on campus."

Q "The girls at UM are cool, but you will find a few of the snobby types—more so here than most places. I made some wonderful friends last year! **The guys are really hot**, but there are a lot of gay men here. Ann Arbor is a very liberal place, and it's very diverse."

Q "We have a bad rep for having really stuck-up people. I won't lie, **Ann Arbor is full of people who are made of money**, but you just have to associate with the type of people you feel comfortable with. Personally, I think that we have a prime selection of really good-looking guys, and most of the girls are nice."

The College Prowler Take On...
Guys & Girls

Although most agree that Michigan isn't known for its hot students, few seem to complain. A handful of students openly admit to not being able to pay attention in class because of the plethora of hotties that surrounds them. At a school as large as UM, you're bound to find, at the very least, a mixed bag when it comes to looks. Luckily, no matter what you prefer, there is most likely somebody sexy on campus just dying to meet you. We may not be on *Playboy*'s top 10 list for hotties, but we're probably not far from an honorable mention, either. Come on, Hugh!

Expect to find good-looking people if you come to the University of Michigan. The majority of the students here take time to look good, and many are on the forefront of the fashion world. Of course, there is always that crazy guy who feels the need to wear shorts when it's 10 degrees outside, and there's a handful of students who go to class in their PJs, but most U of M students look, at the very least, presentable.

The College Prowler® Grade on
Guys: B+

A high grade for Guys indicates that the male population on campus is attractive, smart, friendly, and engaging, and that the school has a decent ratio of guys to girls.

The College Prowler® Grade on
Girls: A-

A high grade for Girls not only implies that the women on campus are attractive, smart, friendly, and engaging, but also that there is a fair ratio of girls to guys.

Athletics

The Lowdown On...
Athletics

Athletic Division:
NCAA Division I

Conference:
Big Ten

School Mascot:
Wolverine

Males Playing Varsity Sports:
393 (3%)

Females Playing Varsity Sports:
372 (3%)

➜

Men's Varsity Sports:
Baseball

Basketball

Cross-Country

Football

Golf

Gymnastics

Ice Hockey

Soccer

Swimming and Diving

Tennis

Track and Field

Wrestling

Cheerleading

Women's Varsity Sports:
Basketball

Cross-Country

Field Hockey

Golf

Gymnastics

Rowing

Soccer

Swimming and Diving

Tennis

Track and Field

Volleyball

Water Polo

Cheerleading

Club Sports:
Alpine Skiing

Men's Boxing

Women's Boxing

Brazilian Jiu-Jitsu

Broomball

Cycling

Figure Skating

Men's Ice Hockey

Women's Ice Hockey

Men's Lacrosse

Women's Lacrosse

Ninjitsu

Roller Hockey

Men's Rowing (Crew)

Men's Rugby

Women's Rugby

Sailing

Shotokan

Soccer

Synchronized Swimming

Tae kwon do

Ultimate Frisbee

Men's Volleyball

Water Skiing

Table Tennis

Intramurals:
3-on-3 Basketball

Broomball

Cross-Country

Golf

(Intramurals, continued)

Flag Football

Ice Hockey

Inner Tube Water Polo

Mini-Soccer

Racquetball

Roller Hockey

Sand Volleyball

Soccer

Softball

Table Tennis

Team Tennis

Tennis

Track and Field

Ultimate Frisbee

Wallyball

Wrestling

Athletic Fields

Michigan Stadium

Kerry Field

Crisler Arena

Canham Natatorium

Yost Ice Arena

Getting Tickets

Every spring, students fill out their football ticket requests, and everyone gets them. The student section is filled with nearly 20,000 students. It ends up costing something like $13 a game, but it's worth every penny. Ice hockey also has tickets that you must pre-purchase, but other events are usually available on a more consistent basis.

Best Place to Take a Walk

The Arb

Best Place to See a Game

Michigan Stadium (the "Big House"), Yost Ice Arena

Most Popular Sports
Football, Ice Hockey, Basketball

Overlooked Teams
Gymnastics, Swimming, Field Hockey, Rowing, Wrestling.

These teams are often ranked high on the national scale. Recently, the women's field hockey team won the National Championship. The men's and women's swimming teams are consistently among the best in the nation, as are the gymnastics teams. Wrestling and rowing are also considered to be Big Ten powerhouses.

Gyms/Facilities

CCRB
This is the most popular student recreation center, complete with basketball courts, an indoor track, a pool, a large weight room, racquetball courts, nearby outdoor tennis courts, and many treadmills, stair-masters, and other fitness machines. Although not sparkling new, its facilities are updated.

NCRB
This newer facility has all the amenities of the CCRB, but it's located on North Campus.

IM Building
Most indoor intramural sports compete here. There are basketball courts, weights, various fitness machines, as well as a large swimming pool.

Students Speak Out On...
Athletics

"IM sports are big here, and it's cool because many IM teams are coed. A lot of people do it just for fun, so competition isn't always a big issue."

Q "Varsity sports are really big on campus. Michigan has a great **reputation for athletic excellence**! Plus, we have the Big House. If you've never seen a Michigan football game, then you won't know what I'm talking about. Michigan stadium is crazy; it's the largest stadium in the United States and holds over 110,000 crazy and screaming fans. IM sports are pretty big, too. I've competed every year that I've been in school!"

Q "Varsity sports are huge here—especially football. Almost everybody goes to the football games, and the overall campus mood is usually an indicator of how well or poor the team played on Saturday. The basketball team is improving, and student support is starting to come around for that. The women's basketball team has been very good, making it to the postseason multiple times in the last few years. Finally, if you come to Michigan, you must go to at least one hockey game. They're so much fun, and **the crowd really gets into it**."

Q "Club sports are great. At a school this big, it's hard to be on the varsity team unless you're a high-school All-American, so club sports are often played at **high levels of competition**, and you get to travel around the country to compete against other college's club teams."

Q "Football is huge at UM. Other than that, you'll hear about other sports, but **football dominates**. I'm not into IM sports, but I know people who are, and they seem to have a lot of fun with them."

Q "Varsity sports are big! I love going to football games; it's so nice to see **so much school spirit**! I'm not too sure about IM sports. I think we have all the basics and some extreme sports as well."

Q "Football is huge—there are over 110,000 people at the home games. **Basketball and hockey are also big**. There are tons of opportunities for IM sports in dorms, frat houses, clubs, and more."

Q "Varsity sports at Michigan are huge! There's nothing in the world like watching a football game in the Big House with 110,000 of your closest friends. **Ice hockey at Yost** is probably even more fun than the Big House, although it only seats 6,000 people. Other sports aren't nearly as popular, but each has its loyal following. IM sports are popular and competitive, so much so that people are willing to sign up for broomball at 2 a.m. during the week."

Q "If you do anything before you graduate, go see a hockey game at Yost. It's insane. **Michigan hockey fans** are often compared to Duke basketball fans. They're crazy!"

Q "Sports on campus are huge, **especially football, basketball, and hockey**. The games are great, so get season tickets to football if you have a chance. Even if you don't use the tickets, it's easy to sell them, usually for a profit. IM sports are also popular."

Q "I think the biggest IM sports are **broomball and inner tube water polo**, both of which are so fun, and both of which I had never heard of before coming here."

The College Prowler Take On...
Athletics

To put it simple, the University of Michigan is a sports fan's paradise. From football to broomball, Michigan's teams are stellar. It's worth going to school here just to experience the Big House packed with over 100,000 maniacal Wolverine fans when the team is in town—especially when we play Michigan State or Ohio State.

At Michigan, the sports teams aren't simply teams, they are a way of life. How could sports not be huge when 110,000 fans fill the biggest stadium in the country on six Saturdays each fall? Although Michigan has two main rivals, Michigan State University and Ohio State, it seems like Michigan is everyone's rival. It's fun to be the school everyone loves to hate, and if you arrive in Ann Arbor having never cheered for the Wolverines, you'll find yourself chanting "Go Blue!" and wearing your maize and blue in no time. In addition to big sports like football and hockey, Michigan's swimming, field hockey, and gymnastics teams, among others, are always among the best in the nation. Intramurals are big, too, and members of winning teams wear their "IM Champion" T-shirts with pride. If you crave both big-time sports and big-time academics, don't even hesitate, come to Michigan.

The College Prowler® Grade on

Athletics: A+

A high grade in athletics indicates that students have school spirit, that sports programs are respected, that games are well-attended, and that intramurals are a prominent part of student life.

Nightlife

The Lowdown On...
Nightlife

Club and Bar Prowler: Popular Nightlife Spots!

The bar scene is very active on Michigan's campus. If you're a true bar rat, here's the schedule down to a science. Rest on Monday. On Tuesday, go to Mitch's. On Wednesday, go to Rick's. On Thursday, go to Scorekeepers. On Friday, go to Touchdown's, and on Saturday most likely back to Rick's. Of course, there are plenty of other bars, but if you want the best drink specials, stick to these spots. Grad students prefer Ashley's and Conor O'Neill's on Main Street, which are Irish pubs.

Ashley's
338 S. State St.
Ann Arbor, MI
Steps from the Diag, Ashley's is a great spot to grab a beer and some great bar food. It's very chill, and usually full of grad students.

Conor O'Neill's
318 S. Main St.

On Main Street, four blocks from campus, is a great Irish pub. Go there for great beer from around the world, but don't expect it to be cheap.

Dominick's
812 Monroe St.

Across the street from the Law Quad sits Dominick's, lauded as one of the favorite bars in town. Only open from March until October, the outdoor patio/garden in the back, and the large outdoor porch in front are packed when the weather is nice. Known for its sangria, great micro brews, and good food, Dominick's is a hit. On a beautiful spring day, expect the place to be packed with students enjoying every second of sunshine they can. It's truly a unique place that is always a great time. Go early, because it closes at 10 p.m.

Mitch's
1301 S. University Ave.

Mitch's is a relaxing bar with live music and cheap Coronas on Tuesday nights.

Rick's
611 Church St.

Just off S. University, across the street from Pizza House sits your typical college basement bar. No one knows why people stand in line just to go to a crowded, dark basement, but it's always a good time. On Wednesdays, drink your fill of $2 pitchers while dancing to the most popular pop/dance songs of the moment.

Scorekeepers
310 Maynard St.

Close to Michigan Theatre, Scorekeepers is hopping on Thursdays, but the best drink specials are on the weekend, when you can get either $2 well drinks or $2 bottles of beer. Good dancing and a good time.

Touchdown Café
1220 S. University Ave.

Close to Mitch's, this bar now hosts some of the best booty-shakin' in town, and it has drink specials to match. Although it was probably a one-night occurence, Eminem (from nearby Detroit), made a surprise guest appearance, and gave a performance that kept the bar open until 4 a.m.

Other Places to Check Out

Bird of Paradise for Live Jazz

Charlie's

Favorite Drinking Games

Flip Cup

Beer Pong

Century Club

Quarters

What to Do if You're Not 21

Go to house parties, drive to Windsor, Ontario, or you can usually get into the Necto; just be prepared to have a big stamp put on your hand by an even bigger bouncer.

Students Speak Out On...
Nightlife

"Michigan has a bar for every occasion and for every night of the week. Touchdown's and Rick's are the places to go if you want to be seen."

Q "**The bar scene at U of M is pretty solid**. It gets kind of old after a while, because you see the same people night in and night out, but that all depends on what you're studying because some people don't have enough time to go to the bar every night. Most bars aren't true dance clubs per se, but they all play good music which gives you the option to dance."

Q "There are some spots where you can get in and be under 21. However, **once you turn 21, there is pretty much a different bar for each night**. On Monday nights, we go to Good Time Charley's; it's more of a restaurant than a bar, but they have good drink specials. It's a good place to chill, shoot pool, or just talk. Tuesday is Mitch's. Very 'Cheers-like' in its atmosphere, but there's a little bit of a dance floor. They usually have a guy with a guitar playing music. He's pretty good, but there are only so many songs that he knows."

Q "There are **lots of bars and clubs on campus**. Scorekeepers is a good one, but it gets old after a while."

Q "There are a lot of bars, but I can't drink, so I don't really know. There are several clubs, but **most people just go to parties**."

Q "On **Wednesday night, you have to go to Rick's**. This is your prototypical college bar. It has big dance floor and places to socialize. The crowd there is very Greek and very jock-ish, although other types of people go there, as well. It's just that you'll see some of the basketball players, football players, and other athletes there a lot. Thursday night is Scorekeepers. It's similar to Rick's in that it is very club-like, but its crowd is more diverse on Thursday nights. They also have $1 Long Islands on Thursday nights, which is a big draw. On Fridays and Saturdays, you usually go to a house party. Not a whole lot of people go out from Sunday to Tuesday, but the weekend usually starts either on Wednesday or Thursday here."

Q "If you are looking for a house party, fraternity party, bar or club, **there is always some place to have a good time on any day of the week**. House parties and fraternity/sorority parties are more who you know, but it is not difficult to find someone who knows someone to get in anywhere. The quantity of bars around campus is limited, however on every given night there is a 'hot spot,' where the majority of students will head. The club scene is rather limited around campus, but if you head to downtown Ann Arbor, Ypsilanti, or Detroit, they are plentiful and always happening."

Q "Touchdown's and Scorekeepers are the main bars. **Studio 4 and Cavern are the clubs we usually go to**. Lately, they have gotten stricter on fake IDs, so if you're not 21, sometimes it's hard. If your ID isn't a 'Michigan,' I wouldn't worry so much."

Q "I live for Dominick's. There is nothing better than spending a spring afternoon **sitting out back with a pitcher of sangria**. It's my favorite bar in Ann Arbor."

Q "I always start out at Charley's for happy hour. At about 10 or 11, we make it to either Rick's, Touchdown's, or Mitch's, which are all right around the same area. The nightlife is great here, although **it tends to get kind of repetitive**."

Q "I'm not 21, so I don't really know about the bars. In terms of clubs, Ann Arbor isn't really a clubbing town. Most kids party at the frat houses or at private parties. There are some clubs in the city, but I haven't really gone to them. **I have heard mixed reviews**. Ann Arbor is close to other cities that have clubs—if you have friends with cars, it's only about a 45-minute drive to the bars in Canada."

Q "I personally don't drink, so I couldn't tell you about the bars, but **my friends said they were pretty standard**."

Q "**Conor O'Neill's is a great Irish bar**, and it's a good break from the scene at the campus bars. The crowd is a bit more mellow, and there is a greater mix of non-students and locals."

Q "Unless you have a flawless fake ID, **bars will pretty much be off limits**. My favorite spot, once I became of age, was Rick's on Wednesday nights. There are not too many clubs in Ann Arbor; there is the Nectarine, the Heidelberg, and the Blind Pig. Your best bet is the frat parties, though."

Q "There are a few really good bars right on campus such as Rick's, Good Time Charley's, and Scorekeepers, but **be prepared to need an ID**."

The College Prowler Take On...
Nightlife

The nightlife in Ann Arbor is fantastic, that is, if you're 21 or older. There are reportedly not a whole lot of bars that will accept that fake ID your friend's older brother got for you, so you're best bet is to find a frat party or house party to drink at. Once you do turn 21 though, the nightlife is pretty active so, until then, start training to go out four nights a week.

There are basically three parts to the social life at Michigan. 1) frats; 2) house parties; and 3) bars and clubs. The bars get good reviews, and they provide a nice escape from the frat scene. If you choose to go Greek, your social life will be dominated by the frat/sorority scene for the first two years. House parties are another viable option, and usually very fun. At Michigan, as opposed to some other schools, you rarely pay for a cup at house parties. Expect to drink for free if there's a keg. Just make sure you return the favor when you throw a party. The bars become a desired option once you're legal. If you're not 21, beware, fake IDs will most likely get taken. Don't worry, your time to "drink like a responsible adult" will eventually come—followed shortly by asprin and other hangover remedies.

B+

The College Prowler® Grade on

Nightlife: B+

A high grade in Nightlife indicates that there are many bars and clubs in the area that are easily accessible and affordable. Other determining factors include the number of options for the under-21 crowd and the prevalence of house parties.

Greek Life

The Lowdown On...
Greek Life

Number of Fraternities:
39

Undergrad Men in Fraternities:
16%

Number of Sororities:
22

Undergrad Women in Sororities:
15%

Fraternities on Campus
(Interfraternity Council):

Alpha Delta Phi
Alpha Epsilon Pi
Alpha Sigma Phi
Alpha Tau Omega
Beta Theta Pi
Chi Phi
Chi Psi
Delta Chi
Delta Kappa Epsilon
Delta Sigma Phi
Delta Upsilon
Kappa Sigma
Lambda Chi Alpha
Phi Delta Theta
Phi Gamma Delta (FIJI)
Phi Kappa Psi
Phi Sigma Kappa
Pi Kappa Alpha
Pi Kappa Phi
Psi Upsilon
Sigma Alpha Epsilon
Sigma Alpha Mu
Sigma Chi
Sigma Nu
Sigma Phi
Sigma Phi Epsilon
Theta Chi
Theta Xi
Zeta Beta Tau

Sororities on Campus
(Panhellenic Association):

Alpha Chi Omega
Alpha Delta Pi
Alpha Epsilon Phi
Alpha Gamma Delta
Alpha Phi
Chi Omega
Delta Delta Delta
Delta Gamma
Delta Phi Epsilon
Gamma Phi Beta
Kappa Alpha Theta
Kappa Kappa Gamma
Pi Beta Phi
Sigma Delta Tau
Sigma Kappa

Multicultural Greek Council (Multicultural Fraternities):

Alpha Iota Omicron Alpha
Kappa Delta Phi
Delta Theta Psi
Lambda Phi Epsilon
Lambda Theta Phi
Pi Alpha Phi
Sigma Lambda Beta
Sigma Lambda Gamma
Zeta Sigma Chi

National Pan-Hellenic Council (Multicultural Sororities):

Alpha Phi Alpha
Delta Sigma Theta
Sigma Gamma Rho
Zeta Phi Beta

Did You Know?

Each year, the Greek community puts on Greek Week, which is a week-long philanthropic event with various competitions between teams of Greek organizations. There is a "**Mr. Greek Week**" competition, as well as Greek Sing and Variety competitions, which pack Hill Auditorium.

Many fraternities and sororities have lavish formals, which often take place as far away as **Chicago and Toronto** for an entire weekend.

Fraternities and sororities pair up each spring for their "pre-parties" the following fall, which take place at fraternity houses before each Michigan home football game. **Don't be surprised if you're dancing to music and drinking beer at 9 a.m.** on a football Saturday. It's a Michigan tradition.

Greek Speak:

Crush Party
This is an event hosted by either a fraternity or a sorority in which a member's date is "crushed" to the party. He doesn't know who has a crush on him until he arrives.

Mixer
A party involving a fraternity and a sorority

Three-way/Four-way
Parties involving multiple Greek houses.

Mud Bowl
A football game between two fraternities (SAE and one other), on Homecoming weekend each year. It takes place on a huge mud field next to SAE's house, and at halftime, two sororities play against each other. It draws a huge crowd, and it is usually televised by ESPN 2 (late-night TV).

Students Speak Out On...
Greek Life

> "The Greek scene provides a lot of opportunities for leadership—either within your house, or through Panhellenic and IFC (Interfraternity Council)."

Q "I'm not really into that stuff, but I have been to some good parties at frats. **Some are cool, some aren't**."

Q "I'm involved in Greek life—it was a really good chance for me to make friends because I didn't know anyone when I got to campus. **It does not dominate the social scene at all**. I have friends who aren't in a house, but it is a big part of campus life."

Q "The social scene is not dominated by the Greek system. Although it is huge and **many freshmen rush**, you do not have to be involved in Greek life to party at the houses. It is really expensive to join, however."

Q "Although pledging wasn't the best, my fraternity brothers are **my best friends** to this day. I wouldn't trade my experience for the world."

Q "I don't think Greek life 'dominates,' but there is **a lot of opportunity**. From my experience, there is a frat or sorority suitable for everyone, but not everyone is in one. For example, none of my friends are, and while it seems dominant at times, it really isn't."

Q "Greek life can be a big part of your life if you let it. It's a little **over 30 percent of the school**, but it can seem much bigger. If you want to get involved, it can be the best time of your career. I never got involved, but I have many friends who are, and most of them love it."

Q "Greek life is certainly a large part of the social scene. As the Ann Arbor bar scene is hard to join until your 21st birthday, the house and **fraternity parties are the way to go**. However, do not think if you are not part of the Greek system you will be lacking in things to do. There are always more than enough options for everyone. One of the great things about Greek life is the opportunity to live in the house your sophomore year. Due to the fact that off-campus housing leases need to be signed in the fall, many first-year students are not quite ready to commit to living with people they have only known for a month or two. Living in a Greek house gives you another entire year before you have to make that decision."

Q "The Greeks at UM are **active but not dominating**. If you don't like Greek life, you can ignore it and come out unscathed. There's more than enough to do with or without it."

Q "The Greek scene is what you make of it. I was in a fraternity, and I was not involved much past my first year. **I found my place elsewhere**."

Q "Greek life is big for certain people. There are many **primarily Jewish houses**, so be prepared. Some sorority parking lots are incredible. I've never seen so many BMWs in my life!"

Q "Greek life at U of M is pretty big. Personally, I didn't get into the frat scene because I really **didn't see a need to pay for friends**. There are a lot of sorority houses to choose from if you are interested. The Greek system doesn't 'dominate' the social scene, but it is a significant part of it."

Q "The Greek scene is **one big community**. If you join your first semester, your life will basically be your house for the first two years of college. Then the frat parties and date parties wear off, and you'll spend your last two years at the bars."

Q "Greek life is prevalent here, but it doesn't dominate the social scene at all. I'm not in a frat, and I've had no problems going to parties, making friends, and having fun. This school is large enough that you can go either way and still have **a great social life**. Although, it is always good to know someone in the Greek system so you can get into their parties."

Q "I've never gotten too involved in Greek stuff. I have a lot of friends in frats and sororities, and **they always have fun parties**. If you're into that stuff, it can be a huge part of your social life. But that's not all there is in terms of having fun and hanging out."

The College Prowler Take On...
Greek Life

Although nearly a decent number of Michigan students are in Greek houses, it doesn't necessarily dominate the social scene, unless, of course, you want it to. Some students think it's a great opportunity to make friends and meet people, while others think it's just too expensive to be worth it—they say they don't need to "buy" friends.

Roughly 20 percent of UM students are involved with Greek life, usually beginning their first semester. Rush takes place mid-way through September, and if one becomes a member, his or her social life is largely dominated by the Greek scene for the first two years. Most students who are members of Greek houses live in a chapter house for their sophomore year. Although the parties used to be more accessible to everyone, the school has cracked down on that recently, and parties are rarely "open" at all. Welcome Week, before classes start in the fall, is when the biggest Greek parties are thrown, and you can usually find huge lines outside of frat houses for a week straight. If you're into it or not, it's, at the very least, worth the experience of going to a huge frat party as a freshman. The first time you go, it's almost surreal, like *Animal House* reincarnated. Get ready to drink cheap, warm beer and sweat more than an Ohio State fan in the middle of the Big House student section.

The College Prowler® Grade on
Greek Life: A

A high grade in Greek Life indicates that sororities and fraternities are not only present, but also active on campus. Other determining factors include the variety of houses available and the respect the Greek community receives from the rest of the campus.

Drug Scene

The Lowdown On...
Drug Scene

Most Prevalent Drugs on Campus:
Marijuana
Ecstasy
Cocaine
Adderall

Liquor-Related Referrals:
432

Liquor-Related Arrests:
355

Drug-Related Referrals:
91

Drug-Related Arrests:
58

Drug Counseling Programs:
CAPS (Counseling and Psychological Services) offers drug counseling programs.

Students Speak Out On...
Drug Scene

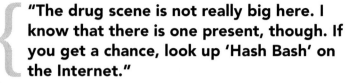

"The drug scene is not really big here. I know that there is one present, though. If you get a chance, look up 'Hash Bash' on the Internet."

Q "There is **a lot of pot floating around** UM. And there are other drugs, but I don't see many of them. It all depends on what type of people you hang out with."

Q "If you're not into drugs, **you won't see them at all**. I haven't, but this doesn't mean drugs don't exist here."

Q "**Some rich sorority girls do coke**, but I've never seen it in my life, nor do I want to."

Q "I can find the drugs I need; UM is **definitely not a dry campus** in that regard."

Q "Ann Arbor is notorious for its **lenient marijuana laws**. Each year, Hash Bash brings the sketchiest people still stuck in the '70s to campus. Beware, they don't smell too good."

Q "I was never into drugs, but **they are prevalent here**. It was never my scene, so I can't really offer you first-hand knowledge of it."

Q "I definitely would not say that there is a drug problem on campus, but I think that if you want to find some, you can usually do it. You just may **have to look around**, unless you're into that scene."

Q "Some people use them, some don't. We do have the infamous Hash Bash, a full day devoted to marijuana on campus. Cops galore! It's more of a festival, though. Pothead or not: it's kind of fun to **be in town for that special day**."

Q "Drugs at UM and Ann Arbor are **available but certainly not overwhelming**."

Q "There are so many different kinds of people here. You'll meet people who have never even seen marijuana, and people who've **snorted enough cocaine to kill a small horse**! It's just like anywhere else: if you look for it, you can find it, whatever 'it' happens to be."

The College Prowler Take On...
Drug Scene

Although the administration and some of the less adventurous students attempt to downplay it, there is a noticeable drug community at University of Michigan. Since "Hash Bash" occurs every spring, and getting caught with pot only results in a small fine, one has to realize that drugs are certainly part of the UM culture. Whether or not there is a huge drug scene is open to debate. The bottom line: drugs are available at U of M, but the majority of the population wisely chooses other avenues of entertainment.

Almost all students agree that if you want drugs, you can most likely find them. Being that most students can comment on the subject, even if they choose not to be involved, only supports the fact that drugs are openly available at U of M. It doesn't seem to be a big problem, but then again, those with drug problems probably won't come out and admit it. While drinking seems to be the popular form of entertainment on campus, some prefer other methods of enjoyment. Either way, you've got to love the fact that thousands of students and vagabonds alike fill the streets of Ann Arbor every spring for a daze-filled day called "Hash Bash." Cheech and Chong would be proud.

The College Prowler® Grade on

Drug Scene: C+

A high grade in the Drug Scene indicates that drugs are not a noticeable part of campus life; drug use is not visible, and no pressure to use them seems to exist.

Campus Strictness

The Lowdown On...
Campus Strictness

What Are You Most Likely to Get Caught Doing on Campus?

• Having liquor in your dorm room

• Trying to get into a bar using a fake ID

Did You Know?

Now a quickly-fleeting Michigan tradition, the "Naked Mile" happens on the night of the last day of classes each winter semester (in April). What used to amount to **hundreds of naked runners and thousands of peeping spectators**, has now been quelled to a few courageous, and often jail-bound, daredevils. Either way, it used to be tolerated by the cops until the University administration cracked down (no pun intended) on it in the past few years. Check out *http://www.nakedmile.com* for more information and racy pictures!

Students Speak Out On...
Campus Strictness

{

**"The Naked Mile is the best thing ever!
Too bad you get arrested now if you try to
run. What's the matter with a little artistic
expression, huh?"**

Q "Campus security is strict in the dorms, but if you're off campus or not in a University building, you can pretty much do whatever you want. Just **watch out for MIPs (minors in possession of alcohol)**. Also, Ann Arbor has lax marijuana laws."

Q "I'd say that **police at UM are pretty lenient**. They usually don't arrest students for getting wasted on campus, and they usually don't go around breaking up parties unless neighbors complain. You can also get away with smoking weed in Ann Arbor with only a $25 fine."

Q "Tickets for minors in possession of alcohol are common, since **being drunk constitutes possession** in Michigan."

Q "**Police are actually pretty cool** about stuff. As long as you aren't being a complete fool, you're fine, although that seems to be a problem for some UM students. Not too many people get in trouble, as far as I know. Parties usually are just asked to keep the extreme noise down. Sometimes they will make people leave, but rarely."

Q "Campus police are pretty cool. They don't give out MIPs **unless you are totally out of control**."

Q "Police and school administration **have really cracked down** on the Naked Mile lately, which I think sucks. It was such a fun tradition, and now it's pretty much over."

Q "Drinking is not hard to do, but **I've had friends get in serious trouble**. Drugs are the same way. It's a college campus, what do you expect?"

Q "Ann Arbor has the most lax marijuana laws I know of. I've heard that **possession is just a small fine**. But if you're an athlete, it depends on your coach and if you're in season. Drugs are definitely out, but some coaches make you have a dry season."

Q "You can definitely get away with drinking in the dorms if you're careful. **I've smuggled many a keg up the Markley stairwells**."

Q "Well, it's easy to get away with a lot, I think, but the University and the city of Ann Arbor have **different laws and penalties**. The University has to follow state laws since it's a public university. If you're caught on campus, chances are you will be treated differently than if you were off campus."

The College Prowler Take On...
Campus Strictness

At Michigan, you have to deal with two authorities: the Ann Arbor police, and Michigan's DPS (Department of Public Safety) who patrol the dorms and campus facilities. If you're smart, you can get away with anything short of murder in the dorms, but be careful. For the most part, the Ann Arbor Police are pretty easy-going, so unless you're out of control, they'll usually leave you alone. They generally seem more concerned with student safety than they are with getting students into trouble.

Campus strictness is not too big an issue at UM. Dorms say they're strict, but you can get away with quite a lot if you're careful. Crafty freshmen can throw some good parties in the dorms, and if they get written up, it's not the end of the world. Frats are pretty conscious about adhering to rules, thus their policies have tightened as of late. Concerning the AAPD, their policies are so lax, it's almost a joke. Any city police force that openly socializes with drunken college kids and imposes an incredibly marginal fine for marijuana use is pretty darn lax. To put this into perspective, students from other colleges would kill to feel as free as students at UM.

B

The College Prowler® Grade on

Campus
Strictness: B

A high Campus Strictness grade implies an overall lenient atmosphere; police and RAs are fairly tolerant, and the administration's rules are flexible.

Parking

The Lowdown On...
Parking

Approximate Parking Permit Cost:
$300

Parking Services:
http://www.parking.umich.edu
umpark@umich.edu

Student Parking Lot?
No

Freshman Allowed to Park?
No

Common Parking Tickets:
$10 ($5 if paid by 5 p.m. of the next business day)
Expired Meter: $10
No Parking Zone: $20
Handicapped Zone: $100
Fire Lane: $15

Parking Permits

Parking permits are few-and-far-between. Since there is no specific student parking lot, one must be crafty (and rich) to get a permit. Most parking facilities are monitored and available only to employees of the University.

Did You Know?

Best Places to Find a Parking Spot
On the street

Good Luck Getting a Parking Spot Here!
State Street during the day

Students Speak Out On...
Parking

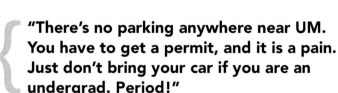

"There's no parking anywhere near UM. You have to get a permit, and it is a pain. Just don't bring your car if you are an undergrad. Period!"

Q "The **parking here is horrendous**. As a freshman, don't bring a car—you won't have anywhere to put it! Sometimes, off-campus housing will have parking, so as you get older, you can decide if you want a spot."

Q "Unless you have some connection, you can't get a permit. However, no one parks in the lots anyways, **just park on the street** (if you can find a spot!)."

Q "No one here drives to class. **Just walk**, and save yourself the hassle."

Q "No one can get an on-campus parking permit until junior year, so **don't count on bringing a car**. Almost no freshman does. If you live in the dorms, it basically won't happen."

Q "This is one of the few drawbacks to living in Ann Arbor. **It's like New York City, parking-wise**. I advise not to bring a car. You won't need it, and you will spend an arm and a leg paying to park. Everything is so close, anyways, and the bus system is great and reliable."

Q "Parking on the street is tough to find, but if you get a ticket at a meter, **it's only $5**."

Q "Parking is horrible! Parking is one of the worst things about campus; **there's never anywhere to park**. They give parking tickets like there is no tomorrow in Ann Arbor."

Q "Parking in Ann Arbor is about knowing the tricks of the trade. If you park in a faculty permit lot or on the street, **you're likely to get a lot of tickets**. But there are some visitor lots where you have to pay a central machine. They rarely patrol those lots, and tickets are cheap."

Q "**Parking is easy if you have a parking pass**. It's brutal if you don't. I'm not sure how much one costs, but if you're in the dorm, it's a good thing to invest in. It is certainly possible to find parking on the streets. I have friends who have done it."

Q "**If you drive to class, you're an idiot**. You'll spend more time looking for a parking spot than you would walking to class."

Q "Parking is horrible on campus. That is one downside to Ann Arbor. If you plan on bringing a car, you can buy a student pass and park in a lot that's probably **miles from where you're staying**. If you have a house or apartment, they usually provide a few parking spots."

The College Prowler Take On...
Parking

Five little letters can accurately summarize the parking situation at UM: S-U-C-K-S. It's expensive, hard to find, and you can't park with a University permit as a freshman. The University permits are not cheap either. On the bright side, if you move into off-campus housing, you'll most likely have a spot to park your car. Otherwise, you're left to fend for yourself finding a spot on the street, which can take hours upon hours. Good luck.

Parking is a huge problem at UM, it's just that simple. Since everyone lives within walking distance, everyone walks to class, but if you must drive, be prepared to hunt for an open meter for quite a while. There are certain lots, but they require a pass to enter, so it's not worth it, and the streets are usually packed bumper to bumper with cars. But not to worry too much, if you get a ticket, you can pay it at the drive-thru window at the police station for $5. And girls, if you catch an officer ticketing your car, be extra charming; you might just get out it.

The College Prowler® Grade on

Parking: D+

A high grade in this section indicates that parking is both available and affordable, and that parking enforcement isn't overly severe.

Transytransportation

The Lowdown On...
Transportation

Ways to Get Around Town:

On Campus
The M-Bus stops every 10 minutes at points scattered throughout South Campus (athletic facilities), Central Campus, and North Campus. For late-night transportation, take the Nite-Owl. For further information, consult Campus Information Center in the Union.

(734) 764-3427

Public Transportation
AATA, The Ride
(745) 996-0400

Taxi Cabs
Ann Arbor Metro
(734) 507-9220

Ann Arbor Taxi
(734) 741-9000

Ann Arbor Taxi Service
(734) 214-9999

Blue Cab
(734) 547-2222

Veterans Cab
(734) 485-7797

Yellow Cab
(734) 663-3355

→

Car Rentals

Alamo
national: (800) 327-9633,
www.alamo.com

Avis
national: (800) 831-2847,
www.avis.com

Budget
national: (800) 527-0700,
www.budget.com

Dollar
national: (800) 800-4000.
www.dollar.com

Enterprise
national: (800) 736-8222,
www.enterprise.com

Hertz
national: (800) 654-3131,
www.hertz.com

National
national: (800) 227-7368,
www.nationalcar.com

Best Ways to Get Around Town

Walk! Or take the University of Michigan Buses.

Ways to Get Out of Town:

Airport

Detroit Metropolitan Airport
(734) AIRPORT
Detroit Metro is only 20 miles away, and approximately 30 minutes from the University of Michigan campus.

Airlines Serving Boston

Air Canada (888) 247-2262,
http://www.aircanada.ca

America West (800) 235-9292,
http://www.americawest.com

American (except int'l arrivals)
(800) 433-7300,
http://www.aa.com

British Airways (800) 247-9297,
http://www.british-airways.com

Continental (800) 525-0280,
http://www.continental.com

Delta Air Lines (800) 221-1212,
http://www.delta.com

Lufthansa (800) 645-3880,
http://www.lufthansa.com

Northwest (800) 225-2525,
http://www.nwa.com

(Airlines, continued)

Southwest (877) 435-9792,
http://www.southwest.com

TWA (800) 221-2000,
http://www.twa.com

United (800) 241-6522,
http://www.united.com

US Airways (800) 428-4322,
http://www.usairways.com

How to Get to the Airport

MSA Airbus
MSAairbus@umich.edu for
reservations
$7 one way, $12 round-trip

Select Ride (734) 663-8898

Ann Arbor Metro Shuttle
(734) 507-9220

Ann Arbor Shuttle Express
(734) 394-1665

A cab ride to the airport
costs $40-50.

Greyhound

The Greyhound Trailways
Bus Terminal is in downtown
Ann Arbor approximately 10
blocks from campus.

For scheduling information,
call 800) 231-2222.

Greyhound Station

116 West Huron

Ann Arbor, MI

Amtrak

The Amtrak Train Station is
near downtown Ann Arbor,
about one mile from the
Union and Central Campus.

For schedule information call
(800) 872-7245.

Ann Arbor Amtrak Station

325 Depot Street

Ann Arbor, MI

Travel Agents

STA Travel, (800) 325-9537

Students Speak Out On...
Transportation

"The airport is really easy to get to, but don't park there. It's really expensive. I would recommend having a friend drop you off."

Q "**Public transportation here is lousy**. The city buses stop running too early. I'm used to public transportation running around the clock. But the campus-wide transportation system is pretty good; it's pretty convenient and free."

Q "Detroit Metro Airport's new terminal is amazing. Since it's a hub for Northwest Airlines, **you can usually find great fares just about anywhere**, and they're non-stop flights."

Q "We have a solid public transportation system here. Campus has buses for anything you need, and **there is a bus system through the city** for off-campus stuff."

Q "Taking the bus to North Campus is a pain, but it's pretty reliable. Supposedly, there are **plans to build a monorail** linking all the sites on campus. They could use it. Ann Arbor has its own buses that go to the mall and grocery stores, but it's always helpful to know someone with a large car."

Q "**I lived off of public transportation** because I have no car, and I thought it was pretty good. I was an expert on predicting the bus schedule."

Q "**Public transportation here is very predictable and quite reliable**. There is the M-bus that just goes around campus (if you live on North Campus, you will be taking this a lot), and there is The Ride which is the city bus that travels through Ann Arbor and some of Ypsilanti."

Q "I made it to graduation without ever riding a University bus, so **I have no idea**."

Q "Honestly, I've always had my own car, so I don't really know. I hear AATA is pretty good. **The University bus system is pretty convenient**, but buses are packed during peak hours and only take you to other parts of campus."

Q "I'm from New York, so as far as I'm concerned, public transportation is lousy. The **city buses stop running at like 7:00 p.m.** Who decided that public transportation shouldn't run around the clock?"

The College Prowler Take On...
Transportation

Overall, U of M students are fairly satisfied with the public transportation system. They feel that the buses run regularly and are, for the most part, safe and clean. This is especially so for the University buses, which are necessary if you live or take classes on North Campus. Students, however, do have one complaint about public transportation: the system does not have the best operating hours. Many students feel that the buses should run later into the night when, arguably, they are needed most.

The University of Michigan bus system is very convenient, and the shuttles run on time. Thousands of students depend on them every day, and the bus system consistently gets good reviews. The public transportation may be another story. With odd hours, and less-than-convenient stops, it may not be worth your time. The best advice: find a friend with a car. Or, then again, unless it's an emergency, there is hardly a reason to leave what's within walking distance, since everything you need is right on campus. Just think about that before you hop on the bus.

The College Prowler® Grade on
Transportation: B

A high grade for Transportation indicates that campus buses, public buses, cabs and rental cars are readily available and affordable. Other determining factors include proximity to an airport and the necessity of transportation.

Weather

The Lowdown On...
Weather

Average Temperature:

Fall:	52 °F
Winter:	26 °F
Spring:	48 °F
Summer:	70 °F

Average Precipitation:

Fall:	2.96 in.
Winter:	2.37 in.
Spring:	3.04 in.
Summer:	3.41 in.

Students Speak Out On...
Weather

"The weather in Michigan can be insane, but it's worth it to go through a Michigan winter because the people are so nice, and the school is the best."

Q "**When it's nice, tons of classes meet outside**. I just love that."

Q "I'm not going to lie; it is cold here. Actually, it fluctuates a lot in the fall and the spring between being really cold and really warm which can be aggravating at times. In the winter, it can get pretty cold, so **make sure that you bring a good jacket**."

Q "This year, we had a really mild winter. Overall, it wasn't bad. This is the first time I have lived in seasons. **Fall is really pretty**. And I think winter is fun because I have never lived in snow. It takes a little time and some warm clothes before you get used to the weather in Michigan, but we're young, so we can handle it."

Q "**Bring a warm jacket and an umbrella**. Actually, the weather is quite bearable. It's beautiful to watch the leaves change color in the fall and see the first growth in spring. If the squirrels can tolerate it, so can we."

Q "The weather is great if you like **a four-season climate**. It gets cold in the winter, but if you're prepared, it's tolerable. The spring and falls are the best because everyone is outside studying, playing Frisbee, and hanging out. Michigan is notorious for its unpredictable weather, so you basically have to be prepared for everything."

Q "If you want good weather, go to school in California. **Have fun during earthquake season**, though!"

Q "I have never been any place with **weather this weird**. Last March, it was 75 degrees for a week, and then it snowed for a week. It's bizarre."

Q "It's cold here, so **be prepared for the winter**. Winter can be very bad! It wasn't too bad this year, but early morning snow makes it easy to start skipping classes, which you don't want to do!"

Q "**Springtime is nice**; Ann Arbor is a very pretty campus. Winter is cold, and it snows a lot here. The campus is huge, so you'll have to take the free bus from one part of campus to the other if you don't want to freeze."

Q "Since the winters are so bad here, Michigan students are not spoiled. So if it's nice out, everyone takes advantage of it. That's a fun part about the fall and spring, **everyone is outside on the Diag** just hanging out."

Q "**The weather around here generally sucks**. The winters are fraught with a lot of snow, whereas the summer sun can sometimes be unbearable. The spring and the fall can be really beautiful, but weather during those months fluctuates too much for you to actually settle on one particular weather pattern. Winter can be horrible because it makes you not want to leave your room. Sitting cooped up in a room for many months during the harsh winter is not my idea of fun."

The College Prowler Take On...
Weather

What did you expect—70s and sunny year round? It's Michigan, for crying out loud! And bad winters are a fact of life here. The weather sucks, but that's no secret. If you're not from Michigan, or even the midwest, you've better be prepared for a winter like you have never dreamed of.

If weather matters that much to you, then you may not be happy at Michigan—at least in the winter. But few places are more pleasant in the fall or spring, when thousands of students crowd the Diag (center of campus) to lay out, toss the Frisbee, or study. Often, however, that awful winter is right around the corner. From about mid-November until late March, don't expect to see the sun much. And it can get downright awful trudging in snow in the bitter cold and freezing rain that is all too common here. Bring a hat, gloves, and a scarf—and don't be embarrassed to wear them. But, if 24,000 students can handle it year after year, so can you. It's really not all that bad. Just let the alcohol warm you up!

The College Prowler® Grade on

Weather: C-

A high Weather grade designates that temperatures are mild and rarely reach extremes, that the campus tends to be sunny rather than rainy, and that weather is fairly consistent rather than unpredictable.

Report Card Summary

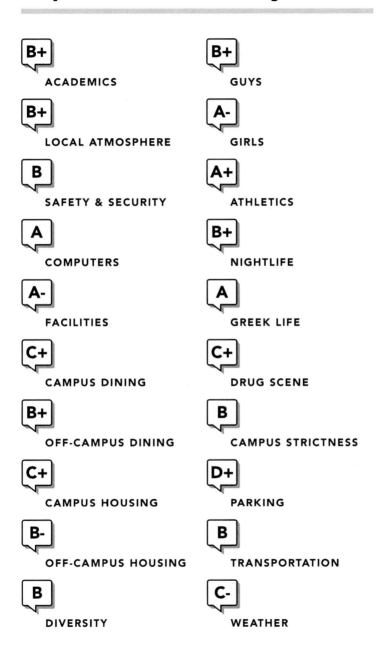

B+ ACADEMICS

B+ LOCAL ATMOSPHERE

B SAFETY & SECURITY

A COMPUTERS

A- FACILITIES

C+ CAMPUS DINING

B+ OFF-CAMPUS DINING

C+ CAMPUS HOUSING

B- OFF-CAMPUS HOUSING

B DIVERSITY

B+ GUYS

A- GIRLS

A+ ATHLETICS

B+ NIGHTLIFE

A GREEK LIFE

C+ DRUG SCENE

B CAMPUS STRICTNESS

D+ PARKING

B TRANSPORTATION

C- WEATHER

Overall Experience

Students Speak Out On...
Overall Experience

{ **"I think Michigan students can be a bit snotty about their school. I'm guilty of it. But if you've got it, you've got it. And Michigan's got it."**

Q "I love this school. I didn't visit before I got here and was a little concerned that I'd be out of place; but **the people here are great**, campus life is wonderful, and you can get involved with almost anything that you want. I know that I'd be miserable at almost any other school."

Q "I wasn't sure if I wanted to go to Michigan before I enrolled. Now I can't see going anywhere else. Michigan provides **the full college experience**, and I couldn't be happier with the time I spent in Ann Arbor."

Q "I love Michigan! I've had the best two years here, and I'm already sad that I only have two more left. I've met the most amazing friends and people. I really enjoy my classes and my major. Overall, **I have no complaints and wouldn't have chosen anywhere else** to spend my college years."

Q "Well, **you will be just a number here**. That was hard for me to adjust to. Ann Arbor is very expensive, especially for out-of-state tuition. It's a nice town and a great atmosphere. However, it can be competitive. Sometimes I ponder what it would have been like if I went to a small, private school. Here, it almost seems like professors are more interested in their research then anything else. But then again, there are the good ones who will stay after office hours and help you out whenever needed. Classes are pretty big—lectures will have tons of people, but labs and discussions are smaller. But if it's a lecture, does it really matter how big the classes are? I'm not a big fan of the grading system, but that also depends on which school you go into."

Q "I've really appreciated being an undergrad at Michigan. The fact that it's **ranked in the top 10 in almost every academic field** means that you can pursue whatever you're interested in at a high level. Trust the source of information. It's also just a great atmosphere for undergrad, in general. There are lots of things to do that help you meet friends and make the huge University seem more like a small community."

Q "I loved it here! It was the best four years of my life. There is nowhere else I would have rather gone. I cannot express to you how much I enjoyed my time here. I came here not knowing anyone; **I left with many caring friends**. My education is first-class, and my friends are excellent. There is nothing more I could have desired from college."

Q "I love this school! I didn't visit before I got here, and I was a little concerned about how I'd like it; but the people here are great, campus life is wonderful, and you can get involved with almost anything that you want. Now I see the world through **maize and blue-colored glasses**. My recommendation would be to pick Michigan and, oh yeah, GO BLUE!"

Q "I loved it here. There were times when **the academic pressure was so much** that I wished I was somewhere else, but I am glad I stuck it out. The engineering school is really good, but really tough, too. The campus is absolutely beautiful, and I had a great time."

Q "Although I was nervous about coming to a big school, I can't imagine having gone anywhere else. My friends from other schools are **always jealous** when I tell them how much fun I have here."

The College Prowler Take On...
Overall Experience

Although many students gripe about the weather, the cost of living, and the calculus GSIs with incoherent accents, one thing holds true: the Michigan experience is one to be envied by all. Students here love their school, and they're not ashamed to say so. Few schools have a greater academic reputation, better sports, and more opportunities for extra-curricular involvement (there are 900 student organizations from which to choose).

Picking a school is a tough decision, and no one expects you to know exactly what you want to do with your life before you've even graduated high school. Fortunately, a school like Michigan can help you find yourself by giving you the chance to try everything under the sun. Nearly every academic area is in the top 10, the sports teams warrant immediate respect, the social life is right with the times, and there are so many ways in which to become involved (it's almost impossible to become a couch potato here). As a Michigan graduate, your degree will be one of the most highly respected in the nation. Graduate schools respect the Michigan name, and undergraduate placement into top schools speaks directly to that fact. And by joining the ranks of the largest alumni population in the world (over 450,000), you'll be a member of a proud family for life. If you choose Michigan, you'll have to try awfully hard to dislike the place after four wonderful years. Join the thousands of maize and blue faithful, and Go Blue!

The Inside Scoop

The Lowdown On...
The Inside Scoop

Michigan Slang

Know the slang, know the school!

The Arb - Nichols Arboretum

Bluebook - An essay exam in which your answers are written in a blue booklet

CRISP - This is an acronym for Course Registration Involving Student Participation. It means registering for classes online.

The Diag - The center of Central Campus; it is the crossroads of campus, bordered by the Grad Library, Mason and Haven Halls, and beautiful lawns full of trees.

Entrée Plus - Money that is stored on your M-Card that can be used at restaurants in campus buildings such as the Michigan Union.

→

Festifall - An event at the beginning of fall semester each year where nearly all of the 900 student organizations set up a table on and around the Diag soliciting new members and involvement; this is a great way to join groups and clubs.

Fishbowl - The Angell Hall computing site.

Group Homework - You'll most likely encounter this first in your calculus class, where certain problems are done in groups and due weekly.

Hash Bash - This happens one Saturday each April. Thousands of students and pot-heads from around the region come to Ann Arbor to celebrate marijuana. Part protest, part festival; it's a sight to be seen.

The Hill - This is a section of campus that houses the majority of first-year students. Residence halls here include Couzens, Alice Lloyd, Markely, Mosher-Jordan (Mo-Jo), and Stockwell.

Maize Craze - The student section at men's basketball games in Crisler arena; students have the best seats in the house and wear maize-colored T-shirts.

Naked Mile - A tradition started by the men's crew team years ago, which involves naked students running through campus on the night of the last day of classes each spring.

Pre-Party - The act of partying before going out to the bars; or, it can be an party before a home football game.

The Rock - This is a giant rock on the corner of Washtenaw and Hill street that is painted practically every night of the year by one group or another for birthdays and other events.

Things I Wish I Knew Before Coming to University of Michigan

- How long and cold winters are

- That the workout facilities weren't quite is good as other Big Ten schools

- How rich the average UM student is

- That almost all freshmen lecture courses are taught by GSIs

- How lenient campus security is

Tips to Succeed at University of Michigan

- Study hard

- Form study groups

- Go to Festifall

- Walk in the Arb

- Paint the Rock

- Get Entrée Plus

- Bring warm clothes

- Be open to new opportunities

University of Michigan Urban Legends

- If you step on the "M" in the center of the Diag, you'll fail your first bluebook exam.

- If you kiss someone under the West Hall Arch at midnight, that's the person you're going to marry.

- The pumas outside the doors of the Natural History Museum only roar on two occasions: when Michigan beats Ohio State in football, and when a virgin graduates from the University.

School Spirit

University of Michigan spirit pervades every inch of the Michigan campus. Few schools have more spirit, especially when it comes to big sports like football and hockey. If you become a Michigan student, you'll soon know the words to the fight song by heart. "The Victors," (once declared "the greatest fight song every written") by America's famous composer, John Phillip Sousa, is played continually at all Michigan sporting events.

Lyrics

"The Victors"

Hail to the victors valiant
Hail to the conquering heroes
Hail, Hail to Michigan
The leaders and best!

Hail to the victors valiant
Hail to the conquering heroes
Hail, Hail to Michigan
The champions of the West!

The Michigan marching band is revered by all and widely considered to be among the best in the nation. Michigan students are not ashamed to wear their maize and blue proudly, and you'll often see many students wearing Michigan gear around campus.

Traditions

The Naked Mile
Although it's been touched on plenty, the Naked Mile is a Michigan tradition that is often emulated on campuses around the country.

Wade in the Water
At orientation, your leader will make you walk through the fountain, just outside of the Michigan League, in the direction of the Diag and the Grad Library. It is a tradition that upon graduation, you walk through the fountain the opposite way, towards Rackham Hall, home of Michigan's Graduate Department.

Finding a Job or Internship

The Lowdown On...
Finding a Job or Internship

The Career Planning and Placement office is an indispensable resource to thousands of Michigan students seeking full-time employment after graduation pr internships during the summers. You can reach the CP&P at *http://www.cpp. umich.edu.*

Each year, hundreds of employers and corporations come to campus to hire Michigan graduates. Michigan attracts the biggest and best companies, and you can find Michigan alumni in any of the world's most prestigious companies. There is a large on-campus interviewing program, in which you may submit your resume to employers on line.

CP&P also offers advising services, workshops, and a reference letter center for Michigan students. Overall, CP&P gets rave reviews from students. For further statistics, visit Michigan Business School's placement Web site at *http://www.bus. umich.edu/StudentCareerServices/PlacementInfo.htm*

Advice

Be on the ball! Search for jobs early, and visit advisors at CP&P for the best advice.

Go to corporate presentations on campus, and introduce yourself to the representatives on campus.

Michigan grads are widely sought-after, and the companies that come to campus expect a lot from students at Michigan. You will find that many corporations that come to Michigan only visit select schools, so consider yourself lucky.

Career Center Resources & Services

Career Exploration

Resume Advice

Pre-professional Services

Graduate School Services

Reference Letter Center

CP&P Library

Job Fairs

Corporate Presentations

Firms That Most Frequently Hire Grads

Ford Motor Company, General Motors, Microsoft, Eli Lilley, Apple Computers, Daimler Chrysler, Intel, Lehman Brothers, Lockheed Martin

Alumni

The Lowdown On...
Alumni

Web Site:
http://www.alumni.umich.edu

Office:
(800) 847-4764

Alumni Publications:
Michigan Alumnus Magazine

Major Alumni Events
The Alumni Center is responsible for organizing the extravagant Homecoming celebrations each year, which involve concerts, lectures, parties, and tailgates—not to mention the football game.

Did You Know?

Famous University of Michigan Alums:

Actors:

Blair, Selma – TV: *Zoe*; Films: *Cruel Intentions*, *Legally Blonde*

Creel, Gavin – Broadway: Tony Nomination for his role in *Thoroughly Modern Millie*

Davis, Ann B. – TV: *The Brady Bunch*; Stage; Films

Elcar, Dana – TV: *MacGyver*, *Baretta*; Films

Gail, Maxwell – TV: *Barney Miller*; Stage; Films

Grier, David Allen – TV: *In Living Color*, *DAG*; Stage: *Dream Girls*, *A Funny Thing Happened on the Way to the Forum*; Films

Jones, James Earl – Films: *Field of Dreams*, voice of Darth Vader in *Star Wars* series, *A Clear and Present Danger*; Stage: *The Great White Hope*, *Fences*

Lahti, Christine – TV: Chicago Hope; Films: *Swing Shift*, *The Doctor*, *Running on Empty*

Letscher, Matthew – TV: *Ellen*, *The Beach Boys*; Films: *The Mask of Zorro*

Liu, Lucy – TV: *Ally McBeal*, *NYPD Blue*, *ER*; Films: *Charlie's Angels*, *Payback*, *True Crime*

Martin, Strother – TV: *Gunsmoke*; Films: *Hud*

McGrath, Bob – TV: *Sesame Street*; Stage; Musician

Mercer, Marian – TV: *Mary Hartman*; Films: *Nine to Five*; Stage: *Promises, Promises*

Nicholas, Denise – TV: *Room 227*, *In The Heat of the Night*; Film: *Ghost Dad*

Paymer, David – Films: *Mr. Saturday Night*, *Quiz Show*, *Get Shorty*, *Payback*

Peters, Jean – Films: *Captain From Castile*, *Three Coins in a Fountain*

Radner, Gilda – TV: *Saturday Night Live*; Films: *Lady in Red*

Sills, Douglas – Stage: *Scarlet Pimpernel*

Art/Design/Architecture:

Donner, Michele Oka – Designed entry to New York City's Hayden Planetarium

Dworsky, Daniel L. – Architect Designed U-M's Crisler Arena

Lane, Kenneth Jay – Fashion jewelry designer/owner of Kenneth Jay Lane, Inc.

Moore, Charles W. – Architect Designed much of the New Orleans World Fair

Robbins, Warren – Art collector whose collection of African art led to the establishment of the Museum of African Art, part of the Smithsonian group

Directors/Writers/Producers, Etc.:

Briley, John – Screenwriter/novelist: *Gandhi*

Brodkin, Herbert – TV producer: *The Defenders, Playhouse 90, Sakharov, Skokie, Holocaust*

Cooper, Hal – TV producer/director: *Maude, Dick Van Dyke Show, Mayberry RFD, That Girl, I Dream of Jeannie, Empty Nest*

Davies, Valentine – Screenwriter: *Miracle on 34th Street*

Hodge, Max – TV writer: *Wild, Wild West, Mission: Impossible, Marcus Welby, The Waltons*

Kasdan, Lawrence – Screenwriter/director: *The Big Chill, Body Heat, Raiders of the Lost Ark, Return of the Jedi, Silverado*

Miller, Arthur – Playwright, stage/films/TV: *Death of a Salesman, The Crucible, The Misfits, Playing For Time*

Newman, David – Screenwriter: *Superman I, II, III, Bonnie & Clyde, What's Up Doc?, Still of the Night*

Newman, Leslie – Screenwriter: *Superman*

Shaye, Robert K. – Producer: *Nightmare on Elm Street,*

Media:

Britt, Donna – Syndicated columnist: *Washington Post*

Dierdorf, Dan – Sportscaster

Elliot, Win – Sportscaster

Fleming, Bill – Sportscaster

Gaines, James Russell – Managing editor: *Time*

Gingrich, Arnold – Founder/publisher: *Esquire*

Guisewite, Cathy – Cartoonist: "Cathy"

Joyce, Andrea – Sportscaster

Kirshbaum, Larry – President, Warner Books

Madigan, John – Publisher, *Chicago Tribune*

Okrent, Daniel – Editor-in-chief, *Life* magazine

Papanek, John – Managing editor: *Sports Illustrated*

Ridder, P. Anthony – President, Knight-Ridder Inc.

Shawn, William – Editor, the *New Yorker*

Simpson, Carole – TV journalist

Wallace, Mike – TV journalist, *60 Minutes*

White, Margaret Bourke – Photographer/journalist

Wilkens, Roger – Journalist, *Washington Post*, shared Pulitzer Prize for Watergate editorials

Wright, Robin – Foreign correspondent

Writers:

Apple, Max – Writer: Free Agents; *Roommates*, *The Air Up There*

Gilbreth, Frank B. – Journalist/novelist: *Cheaper By the Dozen*

Guest, Judith – Novelist: *Ordinary People*

Hopwood, James Avery – Playwright, established the UM Hopwood Awards

MacDonald, Ross – Novelist: *Lew Archer* mystery series

Muller, Marcia – Novelist

Piercy, Marge – Novelist/poet: *Braided Lives*, *Fly Away Home*

Smith, Betty – Novelist: *A Tree Grows in Brooklyn*

Traver, Robert (born John Voelker) – Novelist: *Anatomy of a Murder*

Van Allsburg, Chris – Illustrator/writer: *The Wreck of the Zypher, Jumanji, The Polar Express*

White, Edmund – Journalist/novelist: *Vanity Fair*, the *New Yorker*

Willard, Nancy – Poet/novelist/children's books: *A Visit to William Blake's Inn, Things Invisible to See*

Sports:

Abbott, Jim – Baseball player

Allen, George – Football coach

Berenson, Red – Former pro hockey player, UM hockey coach

Boros, Steve – Former manager, San Diego Padres

Canham, Don – UM track star & former UM Athletic Director

Carter, Anthony – Football player

Conrad, Donald Glover – Owner, Hartford Whalers

Elliott, Chalmers (Bump) – Former UM football coach

Evashevski, Forest – Football player and coach

Ford, William Clay – Owner, Detroit Lions

Freehan, Bill – Baseball player, former UM baseball coach

Gehringer, Charlie – Baseball player

Guthrie, Janet – Race car driver

Harbaugh, Jim – Football player

Harmon, Tom – Football player, Heisman Trophy winner, sportscaster

Hirsch, Elroy – Football player, actor: Unchained

Howard, Desmond – Football player, Heisman Trophy winner

Howard, Juwan – Basketball player

Keating, Thomas Arthur – Football player

Knuble, Mike – Hockey player

Kramer, Ron – Football player

Larkin, Barry – Baseball player

Leach, Rick – Baseball player

Lund, Don – Baseball player

MacPhail, Leland S. – Former president and treasurer, New York Yankees

McCormick, Tim – Basketball player

McKenzie, Reggie – Football player

Mills, Terry – Basketball player

Morris, Hal – Baseball player

Nederlander, Robert – Managing partner, New York Yankees

Ontiveros, Steve – Baseball player

Oosterbaan, Bennie – Football player, former UM football coach

Rickey, Branch – Former president and general manger, Brooklyn Dodgers; brought Jackie Robinson to the major leagues

Riley, Eric – Basketball player

Robinson, Rumeal – Basketball player

Rose, Jalen – Basketball player

Rothenberg, Alan I. – President, Los Angeles Clippers

Russell, Cazzie – Basketball player

Sabo, Chris – Baseball player

Schroeder, John L. – Golfer

Simmons, Ted Lyle – Baseball player

Sisler, George – Baseball player

Sorensen, Lary – Baseball player

Strenger, Richard – Football player

Tomjanovich, Rudy – Basketball player, coach

Wayne, Gary – Baseball player

Webber, Chris – Basketball player

Wilpon, Fred – Chairman of board, New York Mets

Woodson, Charles – Football player, Heisman Trophy winner

Zahn, Geoff – Former baseball player, UM baseball coach

Public Affairs:

Berry, Mary Frances – Chair, Commission on Civil Rights under Carter

Darrow, Clarence – Attorney (Scopes Monkey trial, Leopold-Loeb trial)

Ford, Gerald – President of the United States 1974-77

Matsch, Richard – Colorado federal judge (McVeigh Oklahoma City bombing trial)

Vander Jagt, Guy – Congressman

Wallenberg, Raoul – During World War II, saved thousands of Hungarian Jews by giving them Swedish passports

Wick, Charles Z. – Director of US Information Agency

Astronauts:

Freeman, Theodore

Henize, Karl

Irwin, James B.

Lousma, Jack R.

McDivitt, James A.

White, Edward H.

Worden, Alfred

****Apollo 15**, an all UM space flight, flew to the moon from July 26-Aug. 7, 1971, with astronauts Col. David R. Scott, '49-'50, commander; Maj. Alfred Worden, MS'63, command module pilot; Col. James Irwin, MS'57, lunar module pilot. It was the first expedition with a lunar rover vehicle (used by Scott and Irwin who went to the surface of the moon) and the first flight in which all three astronauts were from the same University. They carried three UM items: a miniature of the UM flag, a miniature of the UM Deptartment of Aerospace Engineering seal, and a charter of the UM Alumni Club of the Moon, which was left on the moon.

Science/Medicine:

Canady, Alexa – Chief of Neurosurgery, Children's Hospital of Michigan

Carson, Benjamin S. – Surgeon, Johns Hopkins

Horwitz, Jerome P. – Organic chemist, synthesized AZT in 1964, a drug now used to treat AIDS

Karle, Isabella Lugoski – Member of National Academy of Sciences; was a member of Manhattan Project

Konopinski, Emil John – Patented device that made first hydrogen bomb with Dr. Edward Teller; worked on the Manhattan Project

Novello, Antonia – First female US Surgeon General

Business:

Bloch, Henry W. – President, CEO, H & R Block, Inc.

del Valle, Manuel Luis – President, Bacardi Corp.

Hockaday, Irvine O. – President, CEO, Hallmark Cards, Inc.

Reins, Ralph E. – President, COO, Mack Trucks, Inc.

Smith, Roger B. – Former chairman, CEO, General Motors

Sperlich, Harold K. – President, Chrysler Corp.

Walgreen, Charles – Founder, Walgreens drugstores

Student Organizations

There are more than 900 student organizations on campus, consult *http://www.umich.edu/clubs.html* for the full list.

ORGANIZATION	TYPE
Alpha Rho Chi	Architecture
Alpine Ski Team	Athletics
Brazilian Jiu Jitsu Club	Athletics
Hockey Club	Athletics
Ultimate Frisbee Club	Athletics
AIESEC	Business and Law
E-Commerce Club	Business and Law
Mock Trial	Business and Law
American Chemical Society Student Affiliates	Chemistry
Alpha Phi Omega Service Fraternity	Community Service
Dance Marathon	Community Service
American Society of Civil Engineers	Engineering and Computing
Solar Car Team	Engineering and Computing
see Greek Life	Fraternities and Sororities
LSA Student Government	Government

Engineering Council	Government
Michigan Student Assembly	Government
Mortar Board	Honor Societies
Phi Beta Kappz	Honor Societies
Black Pre-Medical Association	Medical
Pre-Optometry Club	Medical
African Students Association	Minority and Ethnic
Armenian Students' Cultural Association	Minority and Ethnic
Pakistani Students Association	Minority and Ethnic
Amazin' Blue, coed a cappella	Performance and Literature
Men's Glee Club	Performance and Literature
MUSKET, musical theatre	Performance and Literature
College Republicans	Politically and Socially Active
Amnesty International	Politically and Socially Active
Hillel	Religious
Campus Crusade for Christ	Religious
Hindu Students Association	Religious

The Best
& Worst

Ten Best Things About University of Michigan

1	Football saturdays
2	Lovely Ann Arbor
3	Stellar academics
4	Great social life
5	900 student organizations
6	School spirit
7	Proud reputation
8	Research opportunities
9	Numerous cultural opportunities
10	Academic calendar: school starts in September, and final exams are over before May!

Ten Worst Things About University of Michigan

1 Long and cold winters

2 Overly eccentric GSIs

3 Poor dorm food

4 Outdated residence halls

5 No parking, anywhere!

6 Tuition (most expensive public school)

7 Cost of living

8 UHS

9 Anti-social North Campus

10 So much snow!

Visiting

The Lowdown On...
Visiting

Hotel Information:

University Accomodations:

Bed & Breakfast On Campus
921 E. Huron St.
Ann Arbor, MI
(734) 994-9100
Price: $70-100

Bell Tower
300 S. Thayer St.
Ann Arbor, MI
(800) 562-3559
Price: $100-125

Campus Inn
615 E. Huron st.
Ann Arbor, MI
(800) 666-8693
Price: $100-125

➜

Michigan League
911 N. University Av.
Ann Arbor, MI
(734) 764-3177
Price: $100-125

Hampton Inn South
925 Victors Way
Ann Arbor, MI
(734) 665-5000
Price: $70-100

Other Accomodations:

Comfort Inn
3501 S. State St.
Ann Arbor, MI
(734) 761-8838
Price: $70-100

To Schedule a Group Information Session or Interview
http://www.admissions.umich.edu/visiting

Click on "Schedule your Campus Visit" to reserve your space online. Or, call (734) 764-5692.

Directions to Campus

Driving from the North

- Take US-23 South to M-14 West.
- Follow M-14 West signs closely.
- At the fork, stay to the Right following the "Ann Arbor" signs Take the second exit after the fork, Exit #3, called Downtown Ann Arbor; this will become Main Street.
- Follow Main Street to William Street. Take a left at William Street Continue down William Street until it ends at State St.
- Take a right on State Street. Go one block.
- The Michigan Union is on your right at the intersection of South State Street and South University.

Driving from the South

- Take Washtenaw-Ann Arbor Exit 37B and turn right (west) onto Washtenaw.
- At the fork in the road where Stadium Blvd and Washtenaw split (approximately 2-3 miles), stay to the right on Washtenaw following the Hospital signs.
- Take a left at Hill Street (you'll see "The Rock"). Continue down Hill Street (campus buildings will be on your right).
- Take a right on State Street. Go two blocks.
- The Michigan Union is on your left at the South State Street and South University intersection.

Driving from the East

- Take State Street Exit 177.
- Turn right (north). Continue on State Street approximately 2 miles to the main campus area.

Driving from the West

- Take State Street Exit 177. Turn left (north).
- Continue on State Street approximately 2 miles to the main campus area.

Words to Know

Academic Probation – A suspension imposed on a student if he or she fails to keep up with the school's minimum academic requirements. Those unable to improve their grades after receiving this warning can face dismissal.

Beer Pong / Beirut – A drinking game involving cups of beer arranged in a pyramid shape on each side of a table. The goal is to get a ping pong ball into one of the opponent's cups by throwing the ball or hitting it with a paddle. If the ball lands in a cup, the opponent is required to drink the beer.

Bid – An invitation from a fraternity or sorority to 'pledge' (join) that specific house.

Blue-Light Phone – Brightly-colored phone posts with a blue light bulb on top. These phones exist for security purposes and are located at various outside locations around most campuses. In an emergency, a student can pick up one of these phones (free of charge) to connect with campus police or a security escort.

Campus Police – Police who are specifically assigned to a given institution. Campus police are typically not regular city officers; they are employed by the university in a full-time capacity.

Club Sports – A level of sports that falls somewhere between varsity and intramural. If a student is unable to commit to a varsity team but has a lot of passion for athletics, a club sport could be a better, less intense option. Even less demanding, intramural (IM) sports often involve no traveling and considerably less time.

Cocaine – An illegal drug. Also known as "coke" or "blow," cocaine often resembles a white crystalline or powdery substance. It is highly addictive and dangerous.

Common Application – An application with which students can apply to multiple schools.

Course Registration – The period of official class selection for the upcoming quarter or semester. Prior to registration, it is best to prepare several back-up courses in case a particular class becomes full. If a course is full, students can place themselves on the waitlist, although this still does not guarantee entry.

Division Athletics – Athletic classifications range from Division I to Division III. Division IA is the most competitive, while Division III is considered to be the least competitive.

Dorm – A dorm (or dormitory) is an on-campus housing facility. Dorms can provide a range of options from suite-style rooms to more communal options that include shared bathrooms. Most first-year students live in dorms. Some upperclassmen who wish to stay on campus also choose this option.

Early Action – An application option with which a student can apply to a school and receive an early acceptance response without a binding commitment. This system is becoming less and less available.

Early Decision – An application option that students should use only if they are certain they plan to attend the school in question. If a student applies using the early decision option and is admitted, he or she is required and bound to attend that university. Admission rates are usually higher among students who apply through early decision, as the student is clearly indicating that the school is his or her first choice.

Ecstasy – An illegal drug. Also known as "E" or "X," ecstasy looks like a pill and most resembles an aspirin. Considered a party drug, ecstasy is very dangerous and can be deadly.

Ethernet – An extremely fast Internet connection available in most university-owned residence halls. To use an Ethernet connection properly, a student will need a network card and cable for his or her computer.

Fake ID – A counterfeit identification card that contains false information. Most commonly, students get fake IDs with altered birthdates so that they appear to be older than 21 (and therefore of legal drinking age). Even though it is illegal, many college students have fake IDs in hopes of purchasing alcohol or getting into bars.

Frosh – Slang for "freshman" or "freshmen."

Hazing – Initiation rituals administered by some fraternities or sororities as part of the pledging process. Many universities have outlawed hazing due to its degrading and sometimes dangerous nature.

Intramurals (IMs) – A popular, and usually free, sport league in which students create teams and compete against one another. These sports vary in competitiveness and can include a range of activities—everything from billiards to water polo. IM sports are a great way to meet people with similar interests.

Keg – Officially called a half-barrel, a keg contains roughly 200 12-ounce servings of beer.

LSD – An illegal drug. Also known as acid, this hallucinogenic drug most commonly resembles a tab of paper.

Marijuana – An illegal drug. Also known as weed or pot; along with alcohol, marijuana is one of the most commonly-found drugs on campuses across the country.

Major –The focal point of a student's college studies; a specific topic that is studied for a degree. Examples of majors include physics, English, history, computer science, economics, business, and music. Many students decide on a specific major before arriving on campus, while others are simply "undecided" until delcaring a major. Those who are extremely interested in two areas can also choose to double major.

Meal Block – The equivalent of one meal. Students on a meal plan usually receive a fixed number of meals per week. Each meal, or "block," can be redeemed at the school's dining facilities in place of cash. Often, a student's weekly allotment of meal blocks will be forfeited if not used.

Minor – An additional focal point in a student's education. Often serving as a complement or addition to a student's main area of focus, a minor has fewer requirements and prerequisites to fulfill than a major. Minors are not required for graduation from most schools; however some students who want to explore many different interests choose to pursue both a major and a minor.

Mushrooms – An illegal drug. Also known as "'shrooms," this drug resembles regular mushrooms but is extremely hallucinogenic.

Off-Campus Housing – Housing from a particular landlord or rental group that is not affiliated with the university. Depending on the college, off-campus housing can range from extremely popular to non-existent. Students who choose to live off campus are typically given more freedom, but they also have to deal with possible subletting scenarios, furniture, bills, and other issues. In addition to these factors, rental prices and distance often affect a student's decision to move off campus.

Office Hours – Time that teachers set aside for students who have questions about coursework. Office hours are a good forum for students to go over any problems and to show interest in the subject material.

Pledging – The early phase of joining a fraternity or sorority, pledging takes place after a student has gone through rush and received a bid. Pledging usually lasts between one and two semesters. Once the pledging period is complete and a particular student has done everything that is required to become a member, that student is considered a brother or sister. If a fraternity or a sorority would decide to "haze" a group of students, this initiation would take place during the pledging period.

Private Institution – A school that does not use tax revenue to subsidize education costs. Private schools typically cost more than public schools and are usually smaller.

Prof – Slang for "professor."

Public Institution – A school that uses tax revenue to subsidize education costs. Public schools are often a good value for in-state residents and tend to be larger than most private colleges.

Quarter System (or Trimester System) – A type of academic calendar system. In this setup, students take classes for three academic periods. The first quarter usually starts in late September or early October and concludes right before Christmas. The second quarter usually starts around early to mid–January and finishes up around March or April. The last academic quarter, or "third quarter," usually starts in late March or early April and finishes up in late May or Mid-June. The fourth quarter is summer. The major difference between the quarter system and semester system is that students take more, less comprehensive courses under the quarter calendar.

RA (Resident Assistant) – A student leader who is assigned to a particular floor in a dormitory in order to help to the other students who live there. An RA's duties include ensuring student safety and providing assistance wherever possible.

Recitation – An extension of a specific course; a review session. Some classes, particularly large lectures, are supplemented with mandatory recitation sessions that provide a relatively personal class setting.

Rolling Admissions – A form of admissions. Most commonly found at public institutions, schools with this type of policy continue to accept students throughout the year until their class sizes are met. For example, some schools begin accepting students as early as December and will continue to do so until April or May.

Room and Board – This figure is typically the combined cost of a university-owned room and a meal plan.

Room Draw/Housing Lottery – A common way to pick on-campus room assignments for the following year. If a student decides to remain in university-owned housing, he or she is assigned a unique number that, along with seniority, is used to determine his or her housing for the next year.

Rush – The period in which students can meet the brothers and sisters of a particular chapter and find out if a given fraternity or sorority is right for them. Rushing a fraternity or a sorority is not a requirement at any school. The goal of rush is to give students who are serious about pledging a feel for what to expect.

Semester System – The most common type of academic calendar system at college campuses. This setup typically includes two semesters in a given school year. The fall semester starts around the end of August or early September and concludes before winter vacation. The spring semester usually starts in mid-January and ends in late April or May.

Student Center/Rec Center/Student Union – A common area on campus that often contains study areas, recreation facilities, and eateries. This building is often a good place to meet up with fellow students; depending on the school, the student center can have a huge role or a non-existent role in campus life.

Student ID – A university-issued photo ID that serves as a student's key to school-related functions. Some schools require students to show these cards in order to get into dorms, libraries, cafeterias, and other facilities. In addition to storing meal plan information, in some cases, a student ID can actually work as a debit card and allow students to purchase things from bookstores or local shops.

Suite – A type of dorm room. Unlike dorms that feature communal bathrooms shared by the entire floor, suites offer bathrooms shared only among the suite. Suite-style dorm rooms can house anywhere from two to ten students.

TA (Teacher's Assistant) – An undergraduate or grad student who helps in some manner with a specific course. In some cases, a TA will teach a class, assist a professor, grade assignments, or conduct office hours.

Undergraduate – A student in the process of studying for his or her bachelor's degree.

ABOUT THE AUTHOR

Michael Hondorp currently resides in New York City. Among his many aspirations, he hopes to be involved in higher education administration. He is currently pursuing a role on the Broadway stage. He thanks his friends, his family, and, of course, the University of Michigan for providing him with the experience and education of a lifetime.

E-mail Michael at michaelhondorp@collegeprowler.com with any questions!

Notes

....

....

....

....

....

....

....

....

....

....

....

....

....

Notes

....

....

....

....

....

....

....

....

....

....

....

....

....

Notes

....

....

....

....

....

....

....

....

....

....

....

....

....

Notes

....

....

....

....

....

....

....

....

....

....

....

....

....

Notes

....

....

....

....

....

....

....

....

....

....

....

....

....

Notes

....

....

....

....

....

....

....

....

....

....

....

....

....

Notes

....

....

....

....

....

....

....

....

....

....

....

....

....

Notes

....

....

....

....

....

....

....

....

....

....

....

....

....

Notes

....

....

....

....

....

....

....

....

....

....

....

....

....

Notes

....

....

....

....

....

....

....

....

....

....

....

....

....

Notes

....

....

....

....

....

....

....

....

....

....

....

....

....

Notes

....

....

....

....

....

....

....

....

....

....

....

....

....

Need More Help?

Do you have more questions about this school?
Can't find a certain statistic? College Prowler is
here to help. We are the best source of college
information on the planet. We have a network
of thousands of students who can get the latest
information on any school to you ASAP.
E-mail us at info@collegeprowler.com with your
college-related questions. It's like having an
older sibling show you the ropes!

E-mail Us Your College-Related Questions!

Check out **www.collegeprowler.com** for more details.
1-800-290-2682

Notes

....

....

....

....

....

....

....

....

....

....

....

....

....

Tell Us What Life is Really Like at Your School!

Have you ever wanted to let people know what your school is really like? Now's your chance to help millions of high school students choose the right school.

Let your voice be heard and win cash and prizes!

Check out ***www.collegeprowler.com*** for more info!

Notes

....

....

....

....

....

....

....

....

....

....

....

....

....

Do You Have What It Takes To Get Admitted?

The College Prowler Road to College Counseling Program is here. An admissions officer will review your candidacy at the school of your choice and create a 12+ page personal admission plan. We rate your credentials with the same criteria used by school admissions committees. We assess your strengths and weaknesses and create a plan of action that makes a difference.

Check out **www.collegeprowler.com** or call 1-800-290-2682 for complete details.

Notes

....

....

....

....

....

....

....

....

....

....

....

....

....

Pros and Cons

Still can't figure out if this is the right school for you?
You've already read through this in-depth guide; why not
list the pros and cons? It will really help with narrowing down
your decision and determining whether or not
this school is right for you.

Pros	Cons
....	....
....	....
....	....
....	....
....	....
....	....
....	....
....	....
....	....
....	....
....	....
....	....
....	....

Notes

....

....

....

....

....

....

....

....

....

....

....

....

....

Notes

Get Paid To Rep Your City!

Make money for college!

Earn cash by telling your friends about College Prowler!

Excellent Pay + Incentives + Bonuses

Compete with reps across the nation for cash bonuses

Gain marketing and communication skills

Build your resume and gain work experience for future career opportunities

Flexible work hours; make your own schedule

Opportunities for advancement

Contact sales@collegeprowler.com

Apply now at *www.collegeprowler.com*

Notes

....

....

....

....

....

....

....

....

....

....

....

....

....

Do You Own a Web Site?

Would you like to be an affiliate of one of the fastest-growing companies in the publishing industry? Our web affiliates generate a significant income based on customers whom they refer to our Web site. Start making some cash now! Contact sales@collegeprowler.com for more information or call 1-800-290-2682

Apply now at **www.collegeprowler.com**

Notes

....

....

....

....

....

....

....

....

....

....

....

....

....

Notes

....

....

....

....

....

....

....

....

....

....

....

....

....

Write For Us!
Get Published! Voice Your Opinion.

Writing a College Prowler guidebook is both fun and rewarding; our open-ended format allows your own creativity free reign. Our writers have been featured in national newspapers and have seen their names in bookstores across the country. Now is your chance to break into the publishing industry with one of the country's fastest-growing publishers!

Apply now at *www.collegeprowler.com*

Contact editor@collegeprowler.com or call 1-800-290-2682 for more details.

Notes

....

....

....

....

....

....

....

....

....

....

....

....

....